Preparing Couples For Marriage

A Guide For Pastors
To
Premarital Counseling

Les C. Wicker

CSS Publishing Company, Inc., Lima, Ohio

Library of Congress Cataloging-in-Publication Data

Wicker, Les C., 1943-
    Preparing couples for marriage : a guide for pastors to premarital counseling / Les C. Wicker.
        p. cm.
Includes bibliographical references.
    ISBN 0-7880-1980-5 (pbk. : alk. paper) — ISBN 0-7880-1979-1 (looseleaf, 3-ring binder : alk. paper)
    1. Marriage—Religious aspects—Christianity. I. Title.
    BV835.W52 2003
    259'.13—dc21   2003012506

For more information about CSS Publishing Company resources, visit our website at www.csspub.com or e-mail us at custserv@csspub.com or call (800) 241-4056.

ISBN 0-7880-1979-1 (Binder)
ISBN 0-7880-1980-5 (Book)   PRINTED IN U.S.A.

Table Of Contents

Introduction

Weddings are an important part of the ministry as well as a source of great joy and satisfaction. In the course of my ministry I have conducted over 500 weddings ranging from large church settings, to intimate, quaint services in mountain chapels, to services on the beach. What I have learned from all of this is that every wedding is as different as the people getting married. I have married everyone from professional athletes, to sheriff deputies, to airplane pilots, to concrete truck drivers, to professional photographers. Every wedding experience has brought its own sense of fulfillment in terms of ministry.

I have also found that couples look to the pastor as a source of guidance not only in planning the wedding service, but also in preparation for marriage. The pastor is "the professional" and I believe most pastors undersell themselves at this point. Where else are couples to turn as they not only consider their wedding service, but also make plans for their journey through life?

It is rewarding to participate both in the planning and the celebration of marriage services. The pastor is unique in his/her position of getting to know couples and has an already built-in relationship of trust simply through the pastoral role. Couples are anxious to meet with the pastor and to begin the process of planning. They sometimes approach the initial meeting with uneasiness, not knowing what to expect, yet with a sense of anticipation as they look forward to getting the process underway. Often lasting relationships are formed between the pastor and the couple, and I have found that couples truly treasure this very special bond.

Preparing Couples For Marriage is a comprehensive resource for pastors in their preparatory work with couples planning to be married. It is designed to assist and support the pastor in all aspects of premarital counseling by reviewing the psycho-social-familial past of the prospective bride and groom as well as to examine their compatibility and readiness to assume the responsibilities of marriage. It also serves as a resource for church guidelines, wedding etiquette, rehearsals, wedding music, and the ceremony itself.

No one enters marriage thinking that somehow it will not work out in the end. However, we know that with the many pressures on relationships today, at least one of two marriages will end in separation and divorce. With such alarming statistics, the best thing a pastor can do is to get the couples off to a good start. May this sourcebook serve to that end so that your weddings may be the launching pads for lasting, meaningful, and fulfilling relationships.

My best to you as you prepare couples not only for a beautiful wedding service, but also for their journey in life together.

Les C. Wicker

Acknowledgments

Brief quotes and excerpts have been taken from the following resources with appreciation:

A Country of Strangers, by David Shipler, New York: Alfred A. Knopf, 1997.

"Ask a Rabbi on Jewish Community on Line": Life Cycle Events: Weddings, www.jewish.com

Book of Common Worship, Louisville: Westminster/John Knox Press, 1993.

"The Chancery," The Diocese of Charlotte, Charlotte, North Carolina.

Holy Bible, Revised Standard Version, Division of Christian Education of the National Council of Churches, 1971.

"Marriage Services of the Baptist Church," developed by Rev. Ed Yount, Conover, North Carolina.

"Service of Christian Marriage," *United Methodist Book of Worship,* Nashville: Abingdon Press, 1992.

"Services of Marriage," *The Book of Worship United Church of Christ*, New York: Office of Church Life and Leadership, 1986.

"Why Get Married," by David Freeman, *Theology News and Notes of Fuller Theological Seminary*, December, 1973.

The Knot: www.theknot.com

Contributors

Rev. Joy Baumgartner, Senior Pastor of The United Church of Marco, Marco Island, Florida.

Father James Collins, Pastor of St. Joseph's Catholic Church, Newton, North Carolina.

Laura Hardesty, Wedding Coordinator of Coral Gables Congregational Church, Coral Gables, Florida.

Rev. Thomas Harp, Senior Pastor of Vanderbilt Presbyterian Church, Naples, Florida.

Lee Keene, Wedding Coordinator of Naples United Church of Christ, Naples, Florida.

Janet Middleton, Wedding Coordinator of Naples United Church of Christ, Naples, Florida.

Rev. Thomas Niblock, Senior Pastor of Plymouth Congregational Church, Miami, Florida.

Betty Pursley, Organist of The United Church of Marco, Marco Island, Florida.

Rev. Ted Sauter, Senior Pastor of North Naples United Methodist Church, Naples, Florida.

Dori Smith, soloist of Naples United Church of Christ, Naples, Florida.

Rev. Hayes Wicker, Senior Pastor of First Baptist Church of Naples, Naples, Florida.

Carol Winn, Branch Banking and Trust (BB&T), Newton, North Carolina.

Part I

Foreword

How to Use the Sourcebook

Sessions with Couples

Preparing Couples For Marriage is written as a resource for busy pastors. As it is written by a pastor who understands the many demands in the life of a pastor as well as the need to prepare couples adequately for marriage, it is intended to maximize premarital preparation for the marrying couples and minimize the time requirements for pastors with demanding schedules. Through using the resources of this sourcebook, the marrying pastor has at his/her disposal the source material needful for ensuring that couples receive the proper preparation and guidance for their upcoming marriages.

This sourcebook has been prepared with a large measure of flexibility providing ample resource material for pastors who require several sessions of pre-marital counseling prior to marriage, and at the same time, providing resource material for pastors whose schedules limit their abilities to spend an extended number of interviews with marrying couples, but who wish to be certain that the couples they are marrying have been properly prepared for their upcoming marriage.

The basic structure of the book requires four interviews with couples, which would be an average number of interviews most pastors might require in terms of pre-marital counseling. Pastors who require more one-on-one time with the couple may extend the sessions to seven; pastors who for whatever reason do not find the time for four sessions, may collapse the four sessions into three or two. There are times when pastors are called on to marry couples and there may be time for only one interview. While this is never recommended, out-of-town couples may not be able to make a number of return visits to the pastor. The sourcebook may prove an extremely valuable tool for these more limited interviews in that it allows couples to profile their lives and relationship and even reflect upon it in the absence of the pastor, and at the same time, have the evaluating instrument working for them.

The recommended use of the sourcebook would be as follows:

Seven Sessions:
1. Meeting the Couple and the Developing Relationship
2. Family Profiles
3. Couple Profile
4. Resolving Conflict and Settling Differences
5. Taking Care of Business
6. Faith in the Context of Marriage
7. Reviewing the Marriage Service

Four Sessions:
1. Meeting the Couple and the Developing Relationship
2. Profiling the Marriage: Family Profiles and Couple Profiles
3. Resolving Conflict and Taking Care of Business
4. Faith in the Context of Marriage and Reviewing the Marriage Service

Three Sessions:
1. Meeting the Couple, the Developing Relationship, Family Profile
2. Couple Profile, Resolving Conflict, and Taking Care of Business
3. Faith in the Context of Marriage and Reviewing the Marriage Service

**Note: Time will not allow the pastor to cover every subject. The purpose of handouts is for the couple to review many of their responses together, relying on the pastor only for consultation. Comparing responses will provide an opportunity for the couple to reflect upon themselves, their life journeys, and what they individually will be bringing to the marriage.

Two Sessions:
1. Meeting the Couple, Developing Relationship, Couple Profile
2. Faith in the Context of Marriage and Reviewing the Marriage Service

**Note: Family Profiles, Resolving Conflict, and Taking Care of Business may be offered as handouts with the pastor requesting that couples review their responses between themselves, bringing to the pastor any questions or reflections with which they may need his/her support.

One Session:
The Initial Meeting, the Developing Relationship, and Reviewing the Marriage Service

**Note: Family Profiles, Couple Profile, Resolving Conflict, Taking Care of Business, and Faith in the Context of Marriage, must all be completed privately by the couple as deemed appropriate and needful by the pastor. By taking the time to complete the responses appropriate for these sessions, a couple will gain much insight about themselves, their families, their faith, and the need to take care of their business concerns, and resolve whatever differences that may arise between them.

Special Support and Optional Services

In addition to the resources for premarital interviews mentioned above, this sourcebook has provided the pastor with support for interfaith marriages, racially mixed marriages, and second marriages. Resource materials for these special weddings may be found in the "Optional Sessions" of this sourcebook.

Wedding Resources for the Pastor

The pastor will often want to refer to the valuable materials found in the "Wedding Resources for the Pastor" in the last section of the sourcebook. Included in this chapter are such resources as: Sample Church Guidelines for Weddings, Wedding Guilds/Directors, Wedding Protocol, Wedding Music, Pastoral Letters, and Sample Wills. Some of this material may be duplicated and given to the couple at the initial meeting with the pastor or given by the church wedding coordinator.

Wedding Resources for the Couple

Included with the sourcebook are also important resources that the pastor may copy and give to the prospective bride and groom. Resources here include: Engagement Information, Wedding Customs, Responsibilities of Wedding Party Members, and Wedding Gifts. Providing this information will prove invaluable to couples as well as save them enormous research time. Pastors will soon discover how grateful couples are for having such a valuable resource available.

Biblical Foundations for Marriage

In the Genesis account of creation God created everything and upon its completion God made a pronouncement that it was good. There was a sense of great joy and deep satisfaction over the accomplishments of each day. Light and darkness, land and water, plants and animals, the greater and lesser lights of the heavens, the governance of the seasons, the birds of the air and fish of the sea, were all looked upon in a most positive light as God evaluated all of those facets of creation as very good. Yet when God looked at his final act of creation, the creation of a man, he said, "It is not good for the man to be alone. I will make him a helper fit for him" (Genesis 2:18).

The absence of the woman was the first time God observed anything about creation that was not good, because the man was lonely and there was no one with whom he could share his life. The creation of the woman brought a sense of completeness and oneness to both the man and the woman. In every sense the biblical account affirms the truth that men and women complement each other and one is not complete without the other.

In a poetic sense, this was the first wedding and God was the first to "give the bride away." No wonder *Adam* was leaping for joy and excited beyond words. God had designed and created this beautiful companion and brought her to him. God was the master architect for this magical union we call marriage. It was his idea and he holds the blueprint. It therefore has to be good.

From the very beginning, marriage was viewed as far more than a legally binding contract. It was a gift from God and as such ritually blessed by those in priestly roles and celebrated by family and friends. Not only was it a gift, but also a mystery. "Therefore a man leaves his father and mother and cleaves to his wife and they become one flesh" (Genesis 2:24). Such unions endure not because they are legally bound by law, but because they are unconditional covenants made before God and between two committed people.

The Bible is filled with heart-warming accounts of love and marriage, some almost in storybook form. One of those is the love affair between *Jacob* and *Rachel*. Jacob is actually fleeing from his brother Esau's wrath, when he comes upon Rachel, a shepherdess, who is watering her father's flock. Jacob is immediately taken by her beauty and makes a deal with her father that he will work seven years for her hand. At the end of seven years he is actually given the older daughter, Leah, but refuses to give up in his quest for his beloved Rachel. It takes seven more years of labor, but at long last, he acquires his beloved Rachel.

Moses is raised in the house of Pharaoh and accustomed to the opulent settings of Egyptian royalty. So accustomed, one would have thought he would have chosen a bride from the ranks of royalty, but instead he meets and marries a Midianite shepherd's daughter named *Zipporah*. It is a brief courtship, but a lasting and fulfilling marriage.

Ruth is the faithful and loyal daughter-in-law of Naomi. Naomi and her husband, Elimelech, migrate from Bethlehem to Moab where they, with their two sons, settle in. The two sons marry and one of their wives is named Ruth. As fate and misfortune would have it, Naomi's husband and two sons die, leaving her and her two daughters-in-law widows. Naomi feels it best that she return to Bethlehem, and in an emotional and touching moment urges her daughters-in-law to stay with their relatives in Moab. One decides to stay, but Ruth pleads to accompany Naomi with those memorable words, "Entreat me not to leave you or to return from following you; for where you go I will go, and where you lodge I will lodge; your people shall be my people, and your God my God; where you die I will die, and there will I be buried" (Ruth 1:16). Her loyalty does not go unnoticed as Naomi arranges a meeting between **Ruth** and **Boaz**, a wealthy upstanding townsman and also a kinsman. Boaz recognizes not only Ruth's beauty, but also her character. He is determined to marry her and have her as his own. The union produces a son, Obed, who would be the grandfather of David.

It is noteworthy that the first miracle of Jesus is at a wedding celebration at Cana in Galilee where Jesus, his mother, and the disciples are all guests. Like all weddings, it is a very happy and celebrative setting. Unfortunately the guests consume all the wine, and to be caught without enough wine is quite embarrassing for the bridegroom and his family. When Mary brings the problem to Jesus, he asks those serving to fill the six large water jars with water, and when the task is completed, Jesus changes it to the very finest quality of wine. It is of such quality that the master of the banquet is puzzled at their serving the best wine last. This first miracle of Jesus cannot be eclipsed by the sheer fact of his presence at the wedding. He, along with his mother and his disciples, are into the mix of the celebration. While a very visible guest at Cana, he is always the unseen, but ever-present guest at such happy occasions.

The Apostle Paul compares the relationship of husbands and wives to that of Christ and the church in Ephesians 5:21-33. A couple's relationship with Christ should be infused into the marital bond. They should treat one another with love, honor, and respect out of their reverence for Christ. Paul's analogy is that the church is the bride of Christ and that just as Christ gave himself up for his bride, husbands and wives should give themselves up for one another. Paul refers to the Genesis passage about a man leaving his father and mother and the two becoming one flesh. His reasoning is that if they are one, they should love one another just as they love themselves since the two are actually one flesh.

The approach in I Peter (3:1-9) is that of harmony, understanding, and respect. Peter contends that the behavior of one spouse has great influence over the behavior and actions of the other. He believes that a testy, irritable, complaining, bad-tempered wife will only bring out the worst in her husband. She wins his love as much by the qualities of her inner person as she does by her outward appearance. At the same time Peter does not negate the wife's outward qualities of beauty or her need to address those concerns. In so many ways the two go together and each is a pale reflection of the other. The husband is to love and honor his wife. She is a vessel to be cherished and adored for who she is. Husbands and wives are to be kindhearted and sympathetic toward one another. Neither is to return evil for evil or insult for insult. Just the opposite, they are to respond to their partner's needs with love and affection, knowing this approach is ultimately the better approach and will win in the end.

Settings for Ceremonies

Where should a wedding take place? How does the setting affect the meaning and mood of the service, or does it? Weddings, even Christian faith based weddings, take place in a multitude of settings, not just in the sanctuary of a church, although that is the most probable place. We might say the first wedding took place in a garden setting called Eden when God brought the first bride to the first bridegroom and the bridegroom said,

> "This is now bone of my bone
> and flesh of my flesh;
> she shall be called Woman,
> because she was taken out of the man." (Genesis 2:23)

The description of Solomon's temple in the Book of Kings leads one to wonder if perhaps he were not contemplating a beautiful, sacred setting for some upcoming wedding celebration. Seven years in the building, Solomon barred no holds to ensure that the temple was an exquisitely elegant place of worship. The description of the altar had an extraordinary resemblance to an altar in some modern cathedral where wedding vows might be exchanged.

> "... the golden altar,
> the golden table for
> the bread of the Presence
> the lampstands of pure gold,
> five on the south side and
> five on the north, before the inner sanctuary;
> the flowers, the lamps and tongs of
> gold, basins, wick trimmers, sprinkling bowls,
> dishes and censers." (I Kings 7:48-50)

The places and settings of weddings have been as varied as the couples who have exchanged their vows. Here follows a list of possibilities:

- The main church sanctuary

- The church chapel

- The home of the bride

- The home of the groom

- The home of the pastor

- The church garden

17

- A city's place for elegant events

- The beach

- The mountains

- A college or university chapel

- A park

- A resort

- On board a ship

- On top of a skyscraper

- In a plane

- In a country setting

Part II

Sessions with Couples

Session I

Notes to the Pastor

Session I is the opportunity for the pastor to "Open the Door" with the couple. The first meeting sets the stage for all that follows. During the session the pastor will want to make the couple feel at ease, talk about the premarital process, and review their relationship. This is a *flexible instrument*; thus the points to be considered in each session will depend on whether the pastor is collapsing the number of interviews. "Notes to the Pastor" is included for the convenience of the pastor in determining what he/she might wish to cover without having to review the content of the entire chapter.

Points to Be Considered in Session I

- **Getting to know the couple**

- **Reviewing the process**

- **Answering questions**

- **Reviewing the relationship from the beginning**

Session I

Part A
Meeting the Couple

The initial meeting with the couple is the most important as it sets the tone for the entire relationship between the pastor and prospective bride and groom. This is a time for the pastor to get to know the couple, and thus the importance of making the couple feel at ease cannot be overstated. Little things go a long way in setting the stage for any meeting and paying attention to details ensures success. This first meeting is to get acquainted with the couple, explain the premarital and wedding process, provide needed information concerning guidelines with the given ceremonial setting, and make available the names of resource people who might be involved in the wedding, and also for calendaring in dates for future meetings, the rehearsal, and the wedding itself. Following are some simple tips that will make the most of this initial meeting.

Greeting the Couple

First impressions are often lasting impressions. When the couple first arrives at the pastor's office or place of meeting, the pastor should remember that he/she is both the host and the professional. Here are some ways the pastor can offer an atmosphere of warmth.

Greet the couple in a friendly manner with such opening sentences as:

"I am happy to see you and glad we are going to have some time together."

"I've been looking forward to meeting with you. I know we have lots to talk about."

"We're here to talk about your upcoming wedding, but before we get going with that, I want to tell you how excited I am that you are here. I've heard wonderful things about you."

"Hello, I know you've come for us to talk about your wedding, but before we get started, let's take a few moments to get to know each other."

Make sure the atmosphere is conducive to warmth and productivity by:

- Offering a glass of water, soft drink, or coffee.

- Having the space neat without the abstractions of clutter, leaving the focus on the importance of the present meeting.

- Inviting the couple to be seated together facing the pastor so they have a sense of oneness.

- Seating oneself opposite or perpendicular to the seating of the couple. One should never sit behind a desk as desks create barriers and feelings of authoritativeness. A point to remember is that sitting too close to the couple invades their space, but sitting too far away creates social distance from the couple, equally counter-productive for communication, trust, and exchange.

- Asking the couple if they are comfortable and if you can get anything for them.

- Providing the couple with pen and legal pad for taking notes.

Reviewing the Process

When the pastor senses the couple is at ease, he/she should begin to review the wedding process, including premarital counseling, church guidelines, wedding resource people, wedding budget, place and setting for the wedding, rehearsal, and actual wedding. Usually couples come to the pastor with specific questions they want to ask. Resolving those questions at the outset will enable the couple to focus more on the concerns of the process.

The pastor might initiate the process with any one of the following kinds of statements:

"Now that we have gotten to know each other a little bit, let's go ahead and begin talking about the wedding process. I have some things to share, but before I get started, I know you have some questions. So, let's address your questions before we do anything else."

"We are here to talk about your wedding and I have some things to share with you about the process, but I know you must have come with several questions. I've always found it helpful to put your questions first on the agenda. Do you have anything specifically that you want to talk about?"

"It's good to have this opportunity to review things with you, but before we move on, I know you must have tons of questions. Before we do anything else, let's take a look at your questions."

It is important to respond to each question. Concerns that may seem utterly unimportant to the pastor may have utmost importance to the couple. These may, in fact, be sources of real stress for the prospective bride and groom and getting those resolved at the outset clears the way for the pastor and couple to focus on other concerns without an underlying source of anxiety. The groundwork has been laid for the pastor to outline the premarital and wedding process. He/she may say:

"Now that we have answered your questions, I want to turn our attention to talking about the two of you and how you came to this time and place."

"If you have any other questions, let's take a look at them. If not, I want us to spend a little time talking about the two of you."

Part B
The Developing Relationship

The goal for the pastor here is to enable the couple to explore the journey that has led them to this point and their feelings about each other. As a rule, couples enjoy reviewing the time they have spent in their growing relationship from the time they first met until a decision was made to formalize and solemnize the relationship in the covenant of marriage. Some couples knew each other as children, some were high school sweethearts, some met in college or at work, and some "just happened to meet." Regardless of when or how they met, it has been a joyous and positive journey or else they would not be considering marriage. Reviewing that journey with the couple will not only give them the enriching experience of thinking through what brought them to this time and place, but it will also give the pastor great insight into some of the dynamics of their relationship.

The pastor might begin this part of the session by talking about the importance of relationships and relationship building. The pastor might wonder aloud what it is in the content of personality that simply seems to attract certain people to each other while that attraction has little effect on others. He/she might continue by saying, "What we want to do now is take a look at your relationship and see if we can learn what makes this relationship click, how this relationship is unique, how it began, and how it has become so solid that you want to make it permanent."

Then the pastor may continue the discussion by saying, "I have a few questions that I want to ask the two of you to help you and me understand a little about how you feel about each other and why you decided to be married. I trust you are willing to talk about your relationship and all that has led you to this decision as well as your feelings about one another." Sharing these memories and reflections will serve as an enrichment experience for the couple. Some of these reflections may have never been talked about formally. Couples usually enjoy this time of thinking about their journey together, how they complement each other, and all that has brought them to this time and place. Time will not allow for all the questions, but they serve as starters in enabling the couple to reflect on their relationship.

1. How did the two of you meet?

2. Was there anything unique about the other person that kind of stood out the first time you met?

3. Was it love at "first sight," or did it take a long time for the relationship to warm up?

4. Where were you when you first met each other? Can you remember anything about the place?

5. Who initiated the first conversation?

6. How much time passed from the first time you met until you had contact with each other again?

7. How long have you known each other?

8. Why did you want to go out on a second date?

9. What initially attracted you to your fiancé/fiancée?

10. What did you initially feel you had in common?

11. How often did you see each other during the first weeks of your relationship?

12. When you met each other, were you in another relationship?

13. When you met each other, were you coming out of another relationship?

14. If you were in another relationship, how did you bring closure to that relationship?

15. How do you think this relationship is different from other relationships? What makes this one special?

16. Let's break your relationship into three separate parts which we shall call **The Beginning Sparks**, **The Growing Flame**, and **The Developing Blaze**, and think of some important events or high points in each of those periods of time.

   a. **The Beginning Sparks**

   • During the early days of your relationship, how did you feel?

   • Were you "swept off your feet"? Overwhelmed with joy?

   • Couldn't wait to see him/her again?

   • Did you have to be wooed, convinced, persuaded, won over?

   • What were some of the high and memorable points of the early days?

   • How do you think the relationship rounded the corner to become more than the beginning sparks?

   b. **The Growing Flame**

   • As the relationship developed, did you begin to feel you were in love? Meant for each other?

   • What were some of the important events that made the relationship develop beyond the beginning sparks?

- What things in particular stand out as important to you during this period?

- Did the flame cool any or did it just keep growing?

c. **The Developing Blaze**

- When did you feel the relationship had moved into a serious relationship?

- What was the crowning moment that moved it beyond simply a growing flame?

- Has anything happened in this last period of time that you will always remember?

- When was the final decision made that you should marry and describe the feeling or circumstance?

- Did you formally talk about getting married or did the subject just naturally occur?

- When did you first believe that you would marry him/her?

17. Were there periods of time when you didn't see each other, and how did that make you feel?

18. Was the relationship ever broken off? If so, what do you think was the cause and how were you able to bring things back together?

19. Has there ever been conflict in the relationship and if so, how have you handled it?

20. Name three of your fiancé/fiancée's best qualities and share what makes those qualities special.

    a. _____

    b. _____

    c. _____

21. Would you say your partner gives more than necessary?

22. What are some ways you express appreciation to each other?

23. Do you laugh a lot?

24. If you feel you have shortcomings, do you feel your partner is tolerant?

25. Is your partner your best cheerleader?

26. Who usually makes "the first move"?

    a. Toward conversation?

    b. Toward intimacy?

    c. Toward planning an evening?

    d. Toward reconciliation if there is conflict?

27. Do you ever "keep score"? If so, how can we move the relationship into "give-and-take," accommodating the ups and downs of moods, stress, and feelings?

28. How well do you feel you read one another's body language?

29. In your life journey, do you think you are both "reading from the same book" in your leisure activities? Interests? Intellectual pursuits? Spiritual lives?

30. What role has your faith in God played in your relationship?

31. What do you think makes a couple a winning team?

32. Do you think you "savor every bite" of your relationship? Make the most of every moment?

33. Relationships sometimes have "intruders," such as work, outside hobbies, the internet, friends, nights out on the town, career drive ... Are there intruders in your relationship, and if so, how have you sought to protect your relationship against outside influences?

34. How do you feel your partner validates your life?

35. What does the word "commitment" mean in terms of a relationship?

36. Do you believe that happy couples never have problems?

37. What have you learned from your partner since your relationship began?

38. Do you have fun together?

39. Do you believe for the most part you share the same basic values?

40. If you and your partner do not have the same interests, are you able to enjoy and appreciate the interests of your partner?

41. Do you feel your fiancé/fiancée is romantic? What are some things that give you that feeling?

42. What are some things your partner has done for which you are extremely proud?

43. How has your faith played a part in your relationship?

44. What are you looking forward to about your marriage?

45. What is your fiancé/fiancée's favorite pastime? Meal? Get away place? Relative? Unrealized dream? Music?

46. Can you share a bit about each other's friends? Who are they? Do you also count them as friends? Do you enjoy being around them?

47. Do you have a lot of support for your relationship? What are some of the sources of support? Are there any sources of non-support?

48. What influence has your partner had on your life?

Concluding the Session

The session should conclude with a brief review of subjects covered, a handout of **Groom's** and **Bride's Family Profile** and **Couple Profile** to be filled out and brought to the next session, and a closing prayer which should include some of the subjects covered in today's session.

Sample Closing Prayers

You are the Lord of love and the Giver of all good things, O God. As we reflect on love and marriage and the sheer wonder of the love expressed not only in your love for us, but in the love a man and woman feel for each other, we stand in awe and truly know that every good gift comes from you. Already we feel excitement and joy as we anticipate celebrating this happy event. Walk with these two during these days of preparation and be with them in that blessed event as you were in Cana of Galilee so long ago. Amen.

Lord, many things seem so overwhelming. Right now we are feeling just a little overwhelmed in all that must be done preparing for that wonderful day of celebration. But we know you are the One who not only calms the sea, but who also calms the human heart. Give these your children peace of mind and peace of heart that their wedding will in every way be a time of joy and gladness, not only a blessing to them but for all who share the moments of their joy.

Lord, some time ago a wonderful journey began for N_____ and N_____. It has already been a journey filled with love, joy, hope, and anticipation. That journey has brought them here to this time of planning and preparation for that most glorious day of uniting them as husband and wife. You were with them when the journey began. You will be with them at the altar when their love is confirmed. You will be with them in their journey through life, and you shall be with them even when death shall scatter their days. May they always hold on to you as you always hold on to them. Amen.

Lord, so many things to do, so many people to see, so many places to be, all before we say, "I do." In these days of planning and preparation, breathe a sense of calmness and, yes, even fortitude, into the hearts of these two. We already know their wedding day will be a time that will bless not only their lives, but the lives of all who share their moments of joy. May you be their strength and their guide during these days, and may you be their peace always. Amen.

Lord, you do all things right. Reflecting on our time today, we have come to understand that it was not by happenstance that N_____ and N_____ met some time ago. We thank you not only for bringing their lives together then, but for every step of the journey that has brought them to this time and place and their decision to join their lives in marriage. As you have blessed their journey from its beginning, be their companion and guide in the days that are ahead. Amen.

Holy Christ, as we have reflected on this wonderful love journey between N_____ and N_____ that began these many months ago in their first meeting, we must give you thanks not only for their meeting, but for the bliss and joy of their journey. Remembering not only that first encounter, but the many milestones along the way truly warms the heart. Be in their lives. Be in the love for each other. Be in their hearts forever. Amen.

Lord Jesus, it is moments of reflection like these as we think of all the things that brought N_____ and N_____ to a decision to marry that truly bless the heart and soul. We know that you are in this relationship and have been since the very beginning. As we think about all that has made this journey so special, we can only express our thanks to you for making life good and beautiful through the joy and fulfillment these two have found in one another. Amen.

Sesson II

Notes to the Pastor

Session II takes a look at the families from which the bride and groom come, profiling each in detail. The importance of profiling the couple's families is to enable each to gain a sense of who the future in-laws are. When someone marries a person, he/she also marries the family. Although couples may feel they already know a great deal about their prospective in-laws, putting things on paper allows each to take an objective look at their spouse-to-be's family. This gains understanding and gives perspective.

Points to Be Considered in Session II

- **Who are the bride's and groom's parents?**

- **What kinds of feelings do the bride and groom hold for their parents?**

- **Recollections of childhood**

- **How did each family function?**

Session II

Family Profiles

When we marry a person, we are in essence marrying a history of experience and relationships. Deeply imbedded within each person is a life-long history of experiences from birth to adulthood especially from the most significant people in one's life, his/her family. The world is indeed the "Looking Glass Self," always providing feedback and shaping personality. Even before infants can talk, they receive wordless messages and gather generalized impressions about themselves. They know whether they are lifted or jerked, whether the arms around them are warm and sensitive or vague and distant. They are alert to their mother's moods, her touch, her body movements. Their little radar are extremely sensitive. Thus, the degree of warm responsiveness parents provide forms the foundation for future views of oneself.

Once a child has learned language, a whole new avenue is open for describing his person to himself. Parents are seen as gods and their words are infallible. Words do have power and build or shred self-respect. Imagine the effect of hearing such phrases as: "I can't do a thing with this child," or "I can't wait 'til summer is over and you are back in school," or "You are a pain!" Conversely, the positive stroking we receive as children stays with us in the sense of self-worth and confidence we feel later on. Words of praise build self-respect and the messages we receive as children determine who we are as adults. We are truly our inner child of the past. That is why we can better understand our wife or husband as we know and understand their families and the things that shaped and molded them into who they are.

We must also understand that when we marry a person, we also marry a family, as the quality of relationship between the child and parents will play a significant role the remainder of one's life. The treatment one received growing up, the love that was given or withheld, the self-confidence that was instilled, the values held by the family, and even the sense of self-worth the family held for itself, are all held succinctly within the adult. We are, in every way, an extension of our family, an extension from which no one escapes.

Conflicts often arise when couples fail to understand how the person to whom they are married is really an extension of his/her family. Even though their family may not be perfect, they are still their family. In the mind and heart of one's partner, while their family may no longer be as "gods," they still maintain a very high place of honor and respect. It is next to impossible for a person to abdicate his/her feelings for one's family. Thus, if one's family is denunciated, denunciation is also leveled at the one we love, and that one will often either rise to the defense of his/her family or become defensive within himself. Such is the source of many a marital squabble, and sometimes even demise.

In order for the prospective bride and groom better to understand one another's family, the inventory on page 34 should be given and filled out by each one separately. While lengthy, it will be helpful to the couple to describe his/her family on paper and be able to share that description with their spouse-to-be. The pastor may have given the inventory at the close of Session I, or may now allow time for the couple to privately fill it out. While time will not allow the pastor to review the entire inventory with the couple, the couple should be requested to spend some time together reviewing one another's responses. Couples will gain a great deal of insight about each other simply by filling out and reviewing this inventory.

Concluding the Session

Before ending the session, the pastor should briefly review what has taken place during the interview, and give the couple the handouts to be filled out and brought to the next session. The session may end with a prayer lifting up the special place of importance and honor the two families have had in shaping the lives of the bride and groom.

Sample Closing Prayers

O God, You knew N_____ and N_____ even in their mothers' wombs. You were there when the breath of life came into their being and their parents held them with pride and joy. You were present in the family circle for all the momentous occasions and even those occasions that were not so momentous. Like Mom and Dad, you saw them take their first step, speak their first word, attend their first day of school, and every milestone along the way. Their wedding day will be another milestone in their life journey, and we know you will bless them then as you have blessed them from the very beginning. Amen.

Holy God, it was your idea that we should live in families. You are the giver of families. In times like these we come to understand how important our families are and what great influences they have had on our lives. We would not be who we are without our families. They have guided us, loved us, and given us not only a life, but a faith. As we look before us to our wedding day, we also look behind us to those who have given us far more than we could ever give back. We thank you for all the fond memories of childhood and youth, for parents who believed in us and enabled us to believe in ourselves, and for parents who believed in you and instilled that faith in us. Amen.

Lord, where would we be or what would we be without those who have surrounded us with love and faith from the very beginning? Today we are especially aware and grateful that through your grace we were born into our given families. There is no greater blessing than to have a Christian mother or Christian father who loves us and expresses that love in a life of sacrifice and self-giving. We are here today and who we are today because of them. As we join our lives in marriage and have our own families, may the love and faith they have given be carried forward in and through us. Amen.

Groom's Family Profile

Groom's Father

Father's Name _____ Date of Birth _____

Father's Address _____

How long has your father lived at this address? _____

Other places your father has lived _____

Where did your father grow up? _____

Describe your father's family _____

_____

Would you describe them as close-knit? _____

Are your paternal (father's) grandparents living? _____

If living, where do these grandparents live? _____

Were you close to these grandparents? _____

Father's education _____

Father's occupational career, jobs, positions held _____

_____

Is your father living? _____

What was/is your relationship with your father? _____

_____

Are your father and mother still married? _____

If they are not married, how did the marriage end? _____

If your father and mother are not married, did your father re-marry? _____

How old were you when your father re-married? _____

Briefly describe your relationship with your step-mother _____

_____

Below are some feeling words that may characterize your father. Circle the ones that most clearly describe your father:

Strong	Intelligent	Energetic	Workaholic
Sensitive	A great friend	Protective	Flexible
Reliable	Warm	Witty	Committed
Shy	Athletic	Fun	Thoughtful
Generous	Understanding	Loving	Gentle
Dependable	Approachable	Available	Interested
Honest	Preoccupied	In command	Assertive
Domineering	Affectionate	Great Dad	Visionary

If you become a parent, is there anything you would do different from your father? _____

_____

What do you remember most about your father? _____

_____

Groom's Mother

Mother's Name _____ Date of Birth _____

Mother's Address _____

How long has your mother lived at this place? _____

Other places your mother has lived _____

Where did your mother grow up? _____

Describe your mother's family _____

_____

Would you describe them as close-knit? _____

Are your maternal (mother's) grandparents living? _____

If living, where do these grandparents live? _____

Were you close to these grandparents? _____

Mother's education _____

Mother's occupational career if outside the home _____

_____

Is your mother living? _____

What was/is your relationship with your mother? _____

_____

If your father and mother are no longer married, and your mother re-married, what is your relation-

ship with your step-father? _____

_____

Below are some feeling words that may characterize your mother. Circle the ones that most clearly describe your mother:

Strong	Intelligent	Energetic	Workaholic
Sensitive	A great friend	Protective	Flexible
Reliable	Warm	Witty	Committed
Shy	Athletic	Fun	Thoughtful
Generous	Understanding	Loving	Gentle
Dependable	Approachable	Available	Interested
Honest	Preoccupied	In command	Assertive
Domineering	Affectionate	Great Mom	Visionary

As a parent, is there anything you would do different from your mother? _____

_____

What do you remember most about your mother? _____

_____

Residential History (Places you have lived)

Location   Dates Lived There

_____   _____

_____   _____

_____   _____

_____   _____

Siblings

Brothers: Sisters:

_____   _____

_____   _____

_____   _____

Where did you come in the birth order? _____

Other than small sibling rivalries, were there ever any major points of disagreement or conflicts

between you and any brother or sister? _____

_____

Is there now? _____

Do you feel all children were/are treated equally? _____

Was there/is there competition among your siblings? _____

_____

Was there/is there a brother or sister that you felt/feel closest to? _____

Only Child

Were you the only child? _____

Did you like being the only child or would you have preferred having a brother or sister? _____

_____

Do you feel being an only child gave you more attention? _____

Family Status

How would you describe your family income?

Low Income _____ Middle Income _____ Upper Income _____

How would you describe your family's educational level?

Somewhat Educated _____ Educated _____ Highly Educated _____

How would you describe your family's success level?

Somewhat Successful _____ Successful _____ Very Successful _____

Below are some words that might describe your family's standing in the community or perceptions you feel people may have about your family. Would you circle the five that seem to best characterize these perceptions about your family or home?

Prominent	Involved	Isolated	Respected
Well thought of	Reliable	Had it together	Ideal
Handsome	Low Key	Gathering place	Cultural
Positive	Inviting	Agreeable	Distant
Givers	Good neighbors	Good example	Connected
Strong	Organized	Active	Responsible
Competent	Under stress	Broken	Special
Upstanding	Successful	Popular	Leaders

Has any one of those traits particularly influenced who you are?_____

_____

Recollections

What did you enjoy most about your childhood? _____

_____

What are some activities you did as a family? _____

_____

How did your family celebrate holidays? _____

_____

Did your family take vacations? _____ Was there a particular trip that was particularly

memorable? _____

Did your family support your school activities? _____

Do you feel your parents were your best cheerleaders? _____

Reflecting on your family, who do you think was "Chairman of the Board"? _____

_____

Reflecting on your family, who do you think was the "Heart of the Family"? _____

_____

Were there ever any major family crises in your family? _____

_____

If there were family crises, how were they resolved? _____

_____

Who was your favorite aunt or uncle? _____

What made him/her special? _____

In your growing up years, who outside your family was especially important to you? _____

_____

Do you have a family member that you are especially close to? _____

Have any of your brothers or sisters already left home? _____

How did the family react about their leaving home? _____

_____

Who in your family always helped out when help was needed? _____

_____

Deaths/Grief Experiences

Has your family experienced grief through the loss of family members? _____

_____

How did your family handle the grief experience(s)? _____

_____

Health

Has anyone in your family suffered a serious illness? _____

Has that person fully recovered? _____

How did the illness affect the family? _____

Religion

Is your family active in a church? _____

Members of a church? _____

Have they always been active in a church? _____

Would you say that Christian faith is an important part of your family's life? _____

_____

Did you go to church as a child? _____

How do you think church played an important role in your life? _____

_____

Did your family ask the blessing at meals? _____ Have times of prayer or

devotion?_____

Would you characterize your family as:

Somewhat religious _____ Religious _____ Very religious _____

Who was "the religious leader" of your family? _____

Bride's Family Profile

Bride's Father

Father's Name _____ Date of Birth _____

Father's Address _____

How long has your father lived at this address? _____

Other places your father has lived _____

Where did your father grow up? _____

Describe your father's family _____

_____

Would you describe them as close-knit? _____

Are your paternal (father's) grandparents living? _____

If living, where do these grandparents live? _____

Were you close to these grandparents? _____

Father's education _____

Father's occupational career, jobs, positions held _____

_____

Is your father living? _____

What was/is your relationship with your father? _____

_____

Are your father and mother still married? _____

If they are not married, how did the marriage end? _____

If your father and mother are not married, did your father re-marry? _____

How old were you when your father re-married? _____

Briefly describe your relationship with your step-mother _____

_____

Below are some feeling words that may characterize your father. Circle the ones that most clearly describe your father:

Strong	Intelligent	Energetic	Workaholic
Sensitive	A great friend	Protective	Flexible
Reliable	Warm	Witty	Committed
Shy	Athletic	Fun	Thoughtful
Generous	Understanding	Loving	Gentle
Dependable	Approachable	Available	Interested
Honest	Preoccupied	In command	Assertive
Domineering	Affectionate	Great Dad	Visionary

If you become a parent, is there anything you would do different from your father? _____

_____

What do you remember most about your father? _____

_____

Bride's Mother

Mother's Name _____ Date of Birth _____

Mother's Address _____

How long has your mother lived at this place? _____

Other places your mother has lived _____

Where did your mother grow up? _____

Describe your mother's family _____

_____

Would you describe them as close-knit? _____

Are your maternal (mother's) grandparents living? _____

If living, where do these grandparents live? _____

Were you close to these grandparents? _____

Mother's education _____

Mother's occupational career if outside the home _____

_____

Is your mother living? _____

What was/is your relationship with your mother? _____

_____

If your father and mother are no longer married, and your mother re-married, what is your relation-

ship with your step-father? _____

_____

Below are some feeling words that may characterize your mother. Circle the ones that most clearly describe your mother:

Strong	Intelligent	Energetic	Workaholic
Sensitive	A great friend	Protective	Flexible
Reliable	Warm	Witty	Committed
Shy	Athletic	Fun	Thoughtful
Generous	Understanding	Loving	Gentle
Dependable	Approachable	Available	Interested
Honest	Preoccupied	In command	Assertive
Domineering	Affectionate	Great Mom	Visionary

As a parent, is there anything you would do different from your mother? _____

_____

What do you remember most about your mother? _____

_____

Residential History (Places you have lived)

Location

Dates Lived There

_____   _____

_____   _____

_____   _____

_____   _____

Siblings

Brothers: Sisters:

_____   _____

_____   _____

_____   _____

Where did you come in the birth order? _____

Other than small sibling rivalries, were there ever any major points of disagreement or conflicts

between you and any brother or sister? _____

_____

Is there now? _____

Do you feel all children were/are treated equally? _____

Was there/is there competition among your siblings? _____

_____

Was there/is there a brother or sister that you felt/feel closest to? _____

Only Child

Were you the only child? _____

Did you like being the only child or would you have preferred having a brother or sister? _____

_____

Do you feel being an only child gave you more attention? _____

Family Status

How would you describe your family income?

Low Income _____ Middle Income _____ Upper Income _____

How would you describe your family's educational level?

Somewhat Educated _____ Educated _____ Highly Educated _____

How would you describe your family's success level?

Somewhat Successful _____ Successful _____ Very Successful _____

Below are some words that might describe your family's standing in the community or perceptions you feel people may have about your family. Would you circle the five that seem to best characterize these perceptions about your family or home?

Prominent	Involved	Isolated	Respected
Well thought of	Reliable	Had it together	Ideal
Handsome	Low Key	Gathering place	Cultural
Positive	Inviting	Agreeable	Distant
Givers	Good neighbors	Good example	Connected
Strong	Organized	Active	Responsible
Competent	Under stress	Broken	Special
Upstanding	Successful	Popular	Leaders

Has any one of those traits particularly influenced who you are?_____

_____

Recollections

What did you enjoy most about your childhood? _____

_____

What are some activities you did as a family? _____

_____

How did your family celebrate holidays? _____

_____

Did your family take vacations? _____ Was there a particular trip that was particularly

memorable? _____

Did your family support your school activities? _____

Do you feel your parents were your best cheerleaders? _____

Reflecting on your family, who do you think was "Chairman of the Board"? _____

_____

Reflecting on your family, who do you think was the "Heart of the Family"? _____

_____

Were there ever any major family crises in your family? _____

_____

If there were family crises, how were they resolved? _____

_____

Who was your favorite aunt or uncle? _____

What made him/her special? _____

In your growing up years, who outside your family was especially important to you? _____

_____

Do you have a family member that you are especially close to? _____

Have any of your brothers or sisters already left home? _____

How did the family react about their leaving home? _____

_____

Who in your family always helped out when help was needed? _____

_____

Deaths/Grief Experiences

Has your family experienced grief through the loss of family members? _____

_____

How did your family handle the grief experience(s)? _____

_____

Health

Has anyone in your family suffered a serious illness? _____

Has that person fully recovered? _____

How did the illness affect the family? _____

Religion

Is your family active in a church? _____

Members of a church? _____

Have they always been active in a church? _____

Would you say that Christian faith is an important part of your family's life? _____

_____

Did you go to church as a child? _____

How do you think church played an important role in your life? _____

_____

Did your family ask the blessing at meals? _____ Have times of prayer or

devotion?_____

Would you characterize your family as:

Somewhat religious _____ Religious _____ Very religious _____

Who was "the religious leader" of your family? _____

Session III

Notes to the Pastor

This interview focuses on the couples' feelings and opinions about themselves and their relationship as well as providing objective information about both the bride and groom. The interview is "an analysis of identity," as characterized or revealed by the couple themselves. Sharing such information, either privately with each other or in the presence of the pastor, enables the couple to reflect upon who they are, who their spouse-to-be is, and what each is bringing into the relationship in terms of personal identity.

Points to Be Considered in Session III

- **Personal Identity**

- **Self Evaluation (An Inventory)**

- **Relationship Inventory**

- **Health and Legal Concerns**

Session III

Couple Profile

Couples seeking to solemnize their relationship often feel they know the person they are marrying rather well. Otherwise, they would not be seeking the permanency of legalizing their relationship through marriage. Hopefully, this is true as couples have spent a great deal of time sharing and getting to know one another. By the time the couple comes to the pastor to talk about getting married, many subjects have been covered and identities revealed. They have talked about such concerns as friends and family, favorite foods, places they have been, likes and dislikes, favorite pastime, concerns of the past, and dreams for the future. Such talk is necessary as identity is revealed in the growing relationship. The more couples get to know one another, the more trusting they become in revealing their inner selves and even secrets about themselves they may not be willing to share with anyone else.

All of this is a way of sharing our identity or telling another who we are. We are afraid to tell another who we are until we trust that person enough to reveal who we are. For the most part in life, we are rather guarded about our inner thoughts and feelings. But the more we get to know and trust a person, the more the walls come down and the more comfort we feel in sharing. Couples process this from their very first encounter into years of their marriage. The greater the trust, the greater the freedom one feels to reveal his/her inner person and most private feelings. As this trust develops and grows, truly "the two become as one." There is the freedom to express without fear of rejection.

While couples have informally shared a great deal about themselves and even their most inner feelings, they may not have ever sat down and formally thought about who they are in terms of what each is bringing to the relationship. You have heard the saying, "Put it on paper." Simply put, when we write something down, we are more apt to digest its content fully, analyze it, and absorb it. Writing down such information as biographical data enables us to get an overview of who we are in terms of objective information. Writing things down is informative, even if we feel we know all there is to know about a particular subject, even our own selves.

The **Couple Profile** is simply an informative tool for the pastor to enable couples to reflect formally on who they are in terms of objective data, forced subjective responses, and stated goals and aspirations. It may be one of the few times in life that couples have the opportunity to profile their own lives formally and stand aside and say, "This is who I am." Such profiling is also helpful to the spouse-to-be in terms of gaining insight on the identity of the person to whom one is to be married. In this formal question and answer profile inventory, couples may even say, "I never knew that about you," or they may quietly store something away in their memory bank for future needs and sharing.

The pastor should have given the **Couple Profile** to the couple at the end of the last session and requested that each be filled out and brought to this session. If that has not been done, allow time for the couples to fill out their separate profiles privately.

The pastor is now able to move on with the couple in reviewing their personal profiles. The pastor may want to make a copy of both the groom's and the bride's personal profile in order that all three may visually review it together. Here is the opportunity for the pastor to enable the couple to make observations about themselves, how their lives are similar, and how they are different.

By reviewing such concerns as where each grew up, went to grade or high school, insights will begin to surface. Enable the couple to focus particularly on what "they are bringing to the table," in terms of their life history. They may have entirely different backgrounds. One may be professionally trained with high academic honors in his/her history while the other may have taken a different course. One may have come from a family who did everything together while the other allowed for more solo activities.

There are usually family traditions with regards to holidays. Most often the tradition is steadfast and goes on for years in the same manner. One partner may have the expectation that things will continue as they were, but of course, once married there are two sets of parents, two sets of extended families, and two sets of expectations. By formally reviewing family celebrations, each partner can gain understanding of his/her partner's family traditions, and this should allow each flexibility in meeting the expectations of the other.

Getting couples to talk openly about any unhappiness in childhood is sometimes difficult. The 1 to 10 scale may be a door opener if the pastor notes any clues of unhappiness. Usually people want to remember the good things, which is as it should be. Unfortunately, many grow up in unhappy environments. Not to dwell on it, but to simply to recognize any unhappiness that is noted will enable couples to understand one another better. Past experience defines present behavior and future behavior. Here the effort is to gain understanding of one's future's life experience. Excessive disclosure of unhappiness may signal the pastor to schedule separate conferences with the one who has expressed unhappiness to focus on the causes of the unhappiness and try to work through it so that it does not become a stumbling block for the marriage. If the unhappiness is at a level beyond the professional skill of the pastor, a referral may be in order.

The family table reveals a great deal about the conceptions the couple had of themselves in their developing years. It may reveal such things as authority figures, confidants within the family circle, partnering with siblings or one parent, and the relative degree of importance one may have placed on himself within the family circle.

Getting to know something of the friends of one's childhood, youth, and present is revealing of one's identity. Friends at any age help shape and mold our lives. Sometimes the friends of one's youth carry over into adulthood. One's friends are important and in many ways, like the family, are an extension of one's self. Friends can be great assets, and if not understood, accepted, or included by one's spouse, can also become sources of tension.

One's work is a part of who one is. When people are asked to identify (tell who they are) themselves, often they begin by giving their name and then sharing what they do for a livelihood. We can only conclude that one's work is a very important source describing who we see ourselves to be. If a person has special training for a particular career, the importance of the work is elevated in that a person has spent a number of years and a great deal of effort preparing to be that particular person. It is quite natural that everyone should feel a sense of pride in what they do. Reflective listening on the part of the pastor will go a long way toward underscoring the pride that may be held in a particular job or career. It will also give each partner a renewed sense of appreciation for who the one they are marrying is in terms of work and career.

Health problems are usually, but not always, openly shared by couples who are considering marriage. If health concerns exist, here is a good time to address and process those concerns with the couple. Dealing with these concerns in an open and honest manner will ensure understanding and support later on and also prevent one partner feeling he/she did not know all there was to know about the person they are marrying.

Everyone feels stress at one time or another. Weddings themselves, while sources of great joy, are sources of stress since they are times of transition. Not only are they stressing on the bride and groom, but on their families who are attending to many details. Such simple concerns as "what color the bridesmaid's dresses are to be," may be a source of stress, especially if there is a difference of opinion between a bride and her mom. Other stresses may include moving, leaving home, going from the familiar to the unfamiliar, financial concerns, concern over leaving someone out of the wedding party, and a host of others.

People need to feel good about themselves and they should especially have the admiration of the person they are marrying. Everyone has accomplishments for which they can take pride. It may be completing a degree or obtaining a position. It may even be finding the right person in one's life. Openly acknowledging accomplishments or sources of pride enables one's spouse-to-be to recognize that accomplishment as well.

Life has disappointments and everyone experiences those as well. Like accomplishments, disappointments are a part of who we are. Most tend to safeguard those disappointments way down inside. Men more than women feel sharing disappointments is a sign of weakness and no one wants a "pity party." But perhaps it takes more courage to share them than to hold them inside. We are often afraid that if we share some disappointment we will feel rejection or shame. To the contrary, a strong relationship is able to hear and accept disappointment as well as fortify the one who is disappointed with strength for the future.

By the time couples come to the pastor for premarital counseling, they have already processed such issues as favorite sports, music, and leisure time. Usually, their appreciation for such concerns is quite similar, but not always. They may even have some noted differences. Openly talking about such preferences provides a platform for open dialogue so that preferences are clearly stated.

The Self Evaluation is a battery of true/false statements pertaining to self-image. In reviewing the instrument, the pastor should remember that a good self-image is the basis for giving love, support, and affirmation to others. Loving one's self is the springboard to loving another. When Jesus said to "love your neighbor as you love yourself," he did not mean that we should not love ourselves. Just the opposite. We cannot love another until we love ourselves. While it is assumed that individuals always love themselves, such is not the case. Some people love themselves very little and in fact look upon themselves in a negative way. It is said, "You can't pump from an empty well." Only as a person feels good about himself is he able to give another positive strokes. The pastor should review the Self Evaluation and score, then spend time talking about how good, positive self-love allows one to be a giver of the same.

The Relationship Inventory is a tool to evaluate how the couple relates to one another. It deals with such issues as communication, spending time together, criticism, respect, praise, listening skills, trust, and openness in the relationship. Since the couple has filled out the inventory separately, comparing notes and responses might lend insight to ongoing the functioning of the relationship.

We will cover health and family business matters in another session, but for the moment the Life Profile opens the floor for the couple to begin thinking about health and legal issues.

Concluding the Session

After reviewing the Life Profiles of the bride and groom, the pastor might summarize what the session has been about and highlight anything in particular that has been noted. The pastor should provide the couple with the handout material for the next session. The interview may be closed with a prayer.

Sample Closing Prayers

Lord, here we are today reflecting on our separate lives, how they are in so many ways different and in other ways the same. We come from different families and different communities, and have experienced life in different ways. Yet you brought us together to be of one mind and one heart. We are coming to understand what is meant by the saying, "The two shall become as one." As these two continue to experience life and their love for one another, may they continue to grow as one. Amen.

Eternal God, life is about relationships. Reflecting on N_____ and N_____'s journey through life, we come to understand that many people have helped shape and mold them into who they are today. We thank you for such rich experiences as we have shared, the people who have touched their lives, the friends, the teachers, the influential figures. We know they are better people for having those special individuals embrace and uphold them. We bless you for this time of sharing, the spirit of openness, and the dreams we share for every tomorrow. Amen.

Loving God, what do we have to give each other except our selves, but the gift of the self is truly the greatest gift we have to give. To give one another all that one is or all that one hopes to be is truly the most perfect gift of all. In our time today we have acknowledged some of who we are. Love is giving and love is accepting. May the gifts of giving and receiving find grace and promise as these lives are fulfilled in one another. Amen.

Groom's Personal Profile

Groom's Full Name: _____ Date of Birth _____

Address: _____

How long have you lived at this address? _____

Other places you have lived: _____

Where did you grow up? _____

What high school did you attend? _____

What extra-curricular activities did you participate in during high school? _____

_____

What teacher influenced you the most in high school and why? _____

_____

Higher education or vocational training? _____

Major or special training? _____

Special honors received: _____

Were you ever in the military service? _____

What kinds of activities did your family do together when you were growing up?

    1. As a child? _____

    _____

    2. As an adolescent? _____

    _____

How did you celebrate the holidays?

    1. Thanksgiving: _____

2. Christmas: _____

3. July 4: _____

Measuring your childhood happiness on a scale of 1-10 with 10 being the very happiest, how would you score your childhood?

Not happy   1   2   3   4   5   6   7   8   9   10   Very Happy

The rectangle below represents your family table. Please seat everyone around the table and then draw a line depicting the general lines or flow of communication. Where did you sit and, in particular, what, for the most part, was the flow of communication from you?

Who were your two best friends in elementary school?

1. _____

2. _____

Who were your two best friends in high school?

1. _____

2. _____

Besides your wife-to-be, who are your two best friends now?

1. _____

2. _____

What are some things you enjoy doing with your present friends? _____

_____

How does your wife-to-be enjoy your friends? _____

_____

Where do you work? _____

How long have you worked there? _____

Do you enjoy what you do? _____

What are your career goals? _____

How do you spend your leisure time? _____

Do you feel you have good eating and nutrition habits? _____

Are you in good health? _____

Do you have any health problems? _____

What are some things going on in your life right now that are important to you? _____

_____

Are you under any kind of stress? _____

Who have been the most important people in your life and what influences did they have? _____

_____

_____

What has been your greatest accomplishment? _____

_____

Have there been any major disappointments in your life? _____

_____

What kind of music do you enjoy? _____

What is your favorite sport? _____

What are some ways you work out? _____

Name the two people that you most admire:

1. _____

2. _____

Self Evaluation (T for True — F for False)

_____ I am proud of what I am making of my life.

_____ People generally like me.

_____ I am a loyal person.

_____ I am a flexible person.

_____ I enjoy being around fun people.

_____ I would be a good person to have as a friend.

_____ People trust me.

_____ My family is proud of me.

_____ I believe I will be a good partner in my upcoming marriage.

_____ I am sensitive to people around me.

_____ I am a positive person.

_____ My life is well organized.

_____ I am an honest person.

_____ Life is good.

_____ I am a person of faith.

_____ I am an understanding person.

_____ People can usually count on me.

_____ I usually think of others before I think of myself.

_____ I like my family.

_____ I feel I am able to handle myself in most situations.

Now count the number of T's you marked and add them up.

_____ Total Score. A score of 15 or better would indicate a person has a good self-image and sees himself to be a positive figure in the upcoming marriage.

Relationship Inventory

The following inventory seeks your response to your perceptions of your relationship. Please circle the response that best describes your relationship.

1. We have excellent communication on most every subject.	Yes	No	Sometimes
2. We enjoy spending time with each other's family.	Yes	No	Sometimes
3. We enjoy being alone with each other.	Yes	No	Sometimes
4. We do not criticize each other.	Yes	No	Sometimes
5. We listen to each other's concerns.	Yes	No	Sometimes
6. We accept each other as the other is.	Yes	No	Sometimes
7. If there are differences, we talk things out.	Yes	No	Sometimes
8. Our relationship will always come first.	Yes	No	Sometimes
9. We respect each other's rights.	Yes	No	Sometimes
10. We have similar life goals.	Yes	No	Sometimes
11. We often praise each other's talents, abilities, successes, appearance.	Yes	No	Sometimes
12. We enjoy intimacy with one another.	Yes	No	Sometimes
13. We make an effort to be open and honest about what we are thinking.	Yes	No	Sometimes

14. We are the kind of couple who will work to build a future together.	Yes	No	Sometimes
15. We trust each other.	Yes	No	Sometimes
16. Neither of us tries to control the other.	Yes	No	Sometimes
17. We are comfortable with allowing one another "space."	Yes	No	Sometimes
18. We can usually read each other's feelings.	Yes	No	Sometimes
19. We share a pretty similar philosophy of life.	Yes	No	Sometimes
20. We have an open relationship.	Yes	No	Sometimes

Health and Legal Concerns

Family Physician _____ Dentist _____

Do you have health insurance? _____ With whom? _____

Will both you and your wife be covered? _____

Do you have life insurance? _____

Do you have a will? _____ Have you made arrangements to change the beneficiary

at the time of your marriage? _____

Have you made provisions for your fiancée to be covered in your legal documents? _____

Bride's Personal Profile

Bride's Full Name: _____ Date of Birth _____

Address: _____

How long have you lived at this address? _____

Other places you have lived: _____

Where did you grow up? _____

What high school did you attend? _____

What extra-curricular activities did you participate in during high school? _____

_____

What teacher influenced you the most in high school and why? _____

_____

Higher education or vocational training? _____

Major or special training? _____

Special honors received: _____

Were you ever in the military service? _____

What kinds of activities did your family do together when you were growing up?

   1. As a child? _____

   _____

   2. As an adolescent? _____

   _____

How did you celebrate the holidays?

   1. Thanksgiving: _____

2. Christmas: _____

3. July 4: _____

Measuring your childhood happiness on a scale of 1-10 with 10 being the very happiest, how would you score your childhood?

        Not happy   1 2 3 4 5 6 7 8 9 10   Very Happy

The rectangle below represents your family table. Please seat everyone around the table and then draw a line depicting the general lines or flow of communication. Where did you sit and, in particular, what, for the most part, was the flow of communication from you?

Who were your two best friends in elementary school?

1. _____

2. _____

Who were your two best friends in high school?

1. _____

2. _____

Besides your husband-to-be, who are your two best friends now?

1. _____

2. _____

What are some things you enjoy doing with your present friends? _____

_____

How does your husband-to-be enjoy your friends? _____

_____

Where do you work? _____

How long have you worked there? _____

Do you enjoy what you do? _____

What are your career goals? _____

How do you spend your leisure time? _____

Do you feel you have good eating and nutrition habits? _____

Are you in good health? _____

Do you have any health problems? _____

What are some things going on in your life right now that are important to you? _____

_____

Are you under any kind of stress? _____

Who have been the most important people in your life and what influences did they have? _____

_____

_____

What has been your greatest accomplishment? _____

_____

Have there been any major disappointments in your life? _____

_____

What kind of music do you enjoy? _____

What is your favorite sport? _____

What are some ways you work out? _____

Name the two people that you most admire:

1. _____

2. _____

Self Evaluation (T for True — F for False)

_____ I am proud of what I am making of my life.

_____ People generally like me.

_____ I am a loyal person.

_____ I am a flexible person.

_____ I enjoy being around fun people.

_____ I would be a good person to have as a friend.

_____ People trust me.

_____ My family is proud of me.

_____ I believe I will be a good partner in my upcoming marriage.

_____ I am sensitive to people around me.

_____ I am a positive person.

_____ My life is well organized.

_____ I am an honest person.

_____ Life is good.

_____ I am a person of faith.

_____ I am an understanding person.

_____ People can usually count on me.

_____ I usually think of others before I think of myself.

_____ I like my family.

_____ I feel I am able to handle myself in most situations.

Now count the number of T's you marked and add them up.

_____ Total Score. A score of 15 or better would indicate a person has a good self-image and sees herself to be a positive figure in the upcoming marriage.

Relationship Inventory

The following inventory seeks your response to your perceptions of your relationship. Please circle the response that best describes your relationship.

1. We have excellent communication on most every subject.	Yes	No	Sometimes
2. We enjoy spending time with each other's family.	Yes	No	Sometimes
3. We enjoy being alone with each other.	Yes	No	Sometimes
4. We do not criticize each other.	Yes	No	Sometimes
5. We listen to each other's concerns.	Yes	No	Sometimes
6. We accept each other as the other is.	Yes	No	Sometimes
7. If there are differences, we talk things out.	Yes	No	Sometimes
8. Our relationship will always come first.	Yes	No	Sometimes
9. We respect each other's rights.	Yes	No	Sometimes
10. We have similar life goals.	Yes	No	Sometimes
11. We often praise each other's talents, abilities, successes, appearance.	Yes	No	Sometimes
12. We enjoy intimacy with one another.	Yes	No	Sometimes
13. We make an effort to be open and honest about what we are thinking.	Yes	No	Sometimes

14. We are the kind of couple who will work to build a future together.	Yes	No	Sometimes
15. We trust each other.	Yes	No	Sometimes
16. Neither of us tries to control the other.	Yes	No	Sometimes
17. We are comfortable with allowing one another "space."	Yes	No	Sometimes
18. We can usually read each other's feelings.	Yes	No	Sometimes
19. We share a pretty similar philosophy of life.	Yes	No	Sometimes
20. We have an open relationship.	Yes	No	Sometimes

Health and Legal Concerns

Family Physician _____ Dentist _____

Do you have health insurance? _____ With whom? _____

Will both you and your husband be covered? _____

Do you have life insurance? _____

Do you have a will? _____ Have you made arrangements to change the beneficiary

at the time of your marriage? _____

Have you made provisions for your fiancé to be covered in your legal documents? _____

Session IV

Notes to the Pastor

Conflict is a part of any ongoing relationship, marriage being one among many. Conflicts arise because people have different needs and expectations. Subject matter covered in this interview seeks to enable couples to resolve conflict that comes from the two basic needs: Physical and Psychological. A brief unit on communication skills is provided as a method of reducing conflict. Finally, 27 tips for dealing with conflict are provided as methods of addressing the concern.

Points to Be Considered in Session IV

- **Everyone has needs**

- **Physical needs**

- **Psychological needs**

- **Communication skills**

- **Twenty-seven tips for resolving conflict**

Session IV

Resolving Conflict and Settling Differences

Conflict is a part of any in-depth relationship, marriage being one of longevity in which two people with differing sets of needs come into close physical and emotional contact. No matter what couples may tell you about never having a conflict, conflicts are inevitable and will occur unless one of the people involved never expresses needs, desires, or goals. In the latter case, the conflict is driven inward by the person who is absorbing the hurt by not coming forth with his/her inner feelings and thoughts.

Simply put, people are different. People bring different needs and expectations to the table of mutual exchange in ongoing relationships. It may also be noted that people often have difficulty openly expressing their needs either for fear of rejection or of open confrontation. When feelings are driven underground, they begin to fester and grow and may surface in an uncontrolled manner when they can no longer be contained. Such situations are most unhealthy for relationships as accusations may have been filed or words spoken which cannot be retrieved, causing further hurt and alienation.

It is important for the pastor to implore couples to resolve their conflicts before they develop into full-blown arguments and to equip them with some techniques in conflict resolution. A few simple steps can eliminate huge misunderstandings and keep the relationship fluid and healthy.

Each person brings his/her own set of needs, desires, and goals into the relationship. Conflict arises for two basic reasons: 1) one person's needs or wants are at cross purposes with the other's, and 2) needs are not being met. Defusing differences before they develop is the best antidote for transcending turmoil and allowing the relationship to degenerate into something far less than it is capable of being.

Differences do not simply disappear. They disappear when the concerns of the conflict are addressed and resolved. Couples need a plan to help them resolve differences in an adult and mature manner. Having a plan sends a strong message to the couple that they may expect conflict, but also have a way of resolving it so that the self-worth of neither is damaged and the needs of both are heard.

Physical Needs

Physical needs involve physiological needs, the need for tactile contact, and the need for security or safety. Physiological needs are sometimes characterized as lower level needs, the basic needs for survival, for such things as food, water, and shelter. The need for human contact is a physical need that finds expression in such language as touching, caressing, interaction, nonverbal communication, and human sexuality. The need for security or safety is a feeling that one is protected from forces that may bring pain, be a source of anxiety, or create problems.

Following are some True/False statements which involve physical needs. The inventory seeks responses for how each partner feels about himself/herself as well as how he/she might perceive the partner is feeling. Having introduced the topic of human needs, give the inventory to each partner and allow time for responses.

My Physical Needs

T for True — F for False

_____ My partner makes me feel secure through the non-verbal signals that are sent my way.

_____ I feel my partner would always come to my rescue.

_____ My partner is loyal.

_____ I feel at ease when I am around my partner.

_____ My partner is sensitive to my need to be held and embraced.

_____ I never am concerned about my partner's commitment toward me.

_____ I feel free to express my feelings or opinions to my partner without fear of rejection or confrontation.

_____ My partner welcomes my overtures toward intimacy.

_____ I feel comfortable when my partner caresses me.

_____ I do not believe my partner would abandon me.

_____ When I need reassurance, the first one I turn to is my partner.

_____ My partner never cuts me off at the limb.

_____ My partner stands in my corner.

_____ My partner seeks to meet my physical needs.

_____ My partner is trustworthy.

_____ My partner communicates support.

_____ When I am around my partner, I feel that all is well.

_____ My partner will rally to my support.

My Partner's Physical Needs

T for True — F for False

_____ My partner feels secure around me.

_____ My partner believes I will come to his/her aid.

_____ My partner finds comfort when we embrace.

_____ My partner feels he/she will be received in overtures toward intimacy.

_____ My partner watches for my non-verbal signals of communication.

_____ My partner knows I will rally to his/her support.

_____ My partner is secure in feeling I will not abandon him or her.

_____ My partner knows I am in his/her corner.

_____ My partner knows I am sensitive to his/her physical needs.

_____ When in a crowd, my partner knows I will uphold him/her.

_____ My partner knows I am committed to our relationship.

_____ My partner can disagree with me without fear of retaliation.

_____ My partner trusts me.

_____ My partner knows I will welcome his/her caressing.

_____ My partner knows he/she can count on me.

_____ My partner feels safe when in my presence.

_____ My partner has no fear of rejection.

Psychological Needs

Psychological needs involve the need to relate through close emotional bonds and attachments. They reflect the need to be emotionally connected to another person and to find fulfillment in that relationship. They involve feelings and while no one can control how we feel, sensitivity to our feelings is the basis for growing relationships and the balm for healing when needs have gone unmet. Feelings are real, and whether they are right or wrong, they are still our feelings.

When emotional needs go unmet, a person may respond through expressions of anger or depression. Depression is anger that is turned inward on the self rather than directed toward the source of the anger. Anger comes about for three basic reasons: hurt, fear, and frustration. Hurt may include feelings of rejection, embarrassment, non-approval, or non-support. Fear surfaces when one imagines or foresees those feelings on the horizon. Frustration is one's being overwhelmed or unable to deal with the source of the hurt.

Often people respond to their feelings of anger and frustration by attacking the other person. "You have hurt me so now I am going to hurt you." Retaliation, while a natural response, doesn't usually get the desired results. As a rule, retaliation only deepens the wound and widens the breach of alienation. Retaliation puts the other person on the defense rather than aligning him/her as a partner in finding a solution to the conflict.

Statements of retaliation often begin with the pronoun, "You." Commonly referred to as "You Statements," such statements usually are accusing in nature. "You make me angry." "You are not being honest." "You made that statement and that's that!" "You have no right to say that." You Statements usually arouse anger within the person to whom we are speaking. They feel they are under attack and must defend themselves. The better approach is to make "I Statements," which express how one feels without putting the other person on notice that he/she is the cause of the problem. One might say, "I feel bad when things are not right between us. I don't want you to be angry," or "We need to be as honest as we can. I want things resolved. Can you help me with that?" "I really do understand how you are feeling. Would you allow me to share some of what I am feeling with you? We need to listen and try to get this resolved."

Usually stating your own feelings without attacking the other person is enough to gain the ear and support of that person. When this approach is taken, there is no need to defend, for there is nothing to defend. You have not attacked his/her person; rather, you have positioned him/her to become an ally in resolving the conflict. You are now partners resolving a problem rather than adversaries escalating issues and polarizing yourselves from one another.

Following are some open-ended emotional statements that the pastor should ask the couple to complete. Each should complete the sentence with an emotional/feeling level phrase that supports the psychological/emotional needs of the person and his/her partner. Remind the couple to be careful to use "I Statements," and ones which deal with feelings. Remind the couple they are intending on gaining an ally through the feeling level "I Statement" approach. After the couple has completed the task, discuss how this approach to conflict is much more palatable and will more than likely achieve the desired results, rather than the escalating attack mode.

Concluding the Session

The pastor may conclude the interview by reviewing and summarizing what has been shared in terms of conflict and how to resolve it. The pastor should close the session with a prayer that addresses the need for the intercession of the Holy Spirit when differences arise and need to be resolved.

Sample Closing Prayers

Spirit of God, since the very beginning you have moved over troubled waters and brought peace and calm. You are the Giver of peace and the Settler of differences. Sitting here today, we understand that as surely as we live we will have differences because we are different. It is not our intention to be in denial that differences could never exist. We know they do and will exist, yet we pray that we will never be overcome by any conflict because we know the love of these two will always tear down any wall of separation. Bless N_____ and N_____ as their separate lives become as one. May the indwelling of the Holy Spirit always bring that peace which the world cannot give or take away. Amen.

Lord, the union of N_____ and N_____ in holy matrimony is like the unity candle they shall light that symbolizes their union. The separate flames represent their separate lives. The one flame represents their life joined together. So there is separateness and there is togetherness. Such is life, for we are two yet we are one. Because we are two, at times our own individuality may burn brighter than our unity. Preserve both that we may grow as two and grow as one. May we handle even our differences in such a way that we become stronger in one accord. Amen.

Holy Spirit of God, you are the Great Counselor. You are the One who brings peace and wholeness where there is brokenness and discord. As we anticipate wonderful things for the marriage of N_____ and N_____ and the home they will establish, we are also mindful that even in a setting in which a great love thrives, a setting like this one, differences can create molehills and molehills can become mountains. Give this beautiful couple the will and the wisdom never to allow a difference to fester because we can see today they mean too much to one another. Bless them in every endeavor. Amen.

For the Groom

Meeting Emotional Needs through Positive Communication

(Developing a Communication Style that Works)

Imagine that you and your wife have just had a disagreement that developed into an open conflict. You are both hurt and alienated from one another. Things seem to continue to escalate as you continue to bombard one another with open attacks. The barrage of "You Statements" has put both of you on the defense and now things are rather polarized. Egos are injured, feelings are hurt, and emotions are raw. Rather than salve the wounds, you both have deepened them and poured in the salt. You have become targets for each other's anger, rather than resources for healing. You are holding each other at bay, yet you sense that neither of you really wants the anger or alienation. How can you build a bridge over these troubled waters?

How do you turn this bad situation around? How do you open communication that is positive and healing, rather than accusing and demeaning? It is obvious that there is hurt and the emotional needs of your wife and you have been stepped on. Please complete the following sentences by using "I Statements," that would de-escalate the conflict and at the same time meet the emotional needs of your wife whom you love.

You know, dear, when we argue I feel _____

I am feeling distant right now. Would you _____

When we argue, we seem to lose _____

I feel we are hurting each other; let's _____

I am not comfortable with how things are going and I don't feel you are comfortable either. Can

we _____

When I am included in your plans, I feel _____

I know we are both hurting right now. Let's _____

I feel special when _____

I feel close to you when _____

It makes me feel good when _____

Knowing we can talk through things makes me feel _____

For the Bride

Meeting Emotional Needs through Positive Communication

(Developing a Communication Style that Works)

Imagine that you and your husband have just had a disagreement that developed into an open conflict. You are both hurt and alienated from one another. Things seem to continue to escalate as you continue to bombard one another with open attacks. The barrage of "You Statements" have put both of you on the defense and now things are rather polarized. Egos are injured, feelings are hurt, and emotions are raw. Rather than salve the wounds, you both have deepened them and poured in the salt. You have become targets for each other's anger, rather than resources for healing. You are holding each other at bay, yet you sense that neither of you really wants the anger or alienation. How can you build a bridge over these troubled waters?

How do you turn this bad situation around? How do you open communication that is positive and healing, rather than accusing and demeaning? It is obvious that there is hurt and the emotional needs of your husband and you have been stepped on. Please complete the following sentences by using "I Statements," that would de-escalate the conflict and at the same time meet the emotional needs of your husband whom you love.

You know, dear, when we argue I feel _____

I am feeling distant right now. Would you _____

When we argue, we seem to lose _____

I feel we are hurting each other; let's _____

I am not comfortable with how things are going and I don't feel you are comfortable either. Can

we _____

When I am included in your plans, I feel _____

I know we are both hurting right now. Let's _____

I feel special when _____

I feel close to you when _____

It makes me feel good when _____

Knowing we can talk through things makes me feel _____

76

Conflict Busting

(Tips for Building Bridges Rather Than Walls)

1. **Get Started.** Someone said that getting started is half the job. This holds true more in solving conflict that any other endeavor. Let's admit that it is hard to get started, but once the ice toward reconciliation is broken, it is downhill all the way from there. Sometimes just one gesture does the trick. Go ahead and swallow your pride, reach out and touch, extend a hand, give a hug, just make the first move and see what follows! Usually the loved one is just as anxious as you to put things to rest, but no one is willing to make the first move. Don't allow conflict to become a power struggle because power struggles don't move relationships any where but downhill. Walls will begin to fall when we are willing to make the first move on the road to reconciliation.

2. **Fantasize — Don't Criticize.** Envision good things between you and your partner. Remember the good experiences of the past and understand that it can be that way again and soon. Try not to throw darts because darts only hurt and escalate our partner's defenses. Being logical and reminding yourself and your partner what is happening lowers the tension level. Remember some wonderful experience you have had together and make that experience the subject of conversation. Even fantasize about some future happy experience together.

3. **Reach Out and Touch.** Reach out and touch, so the phone company says. Great advice, especially when two people are experiencing conflict. Go ahead and do it literally! It's really difficult to speak harshly to someone when we are touching him/her or they are touching us. Touching has a calming effect. Touching expresses love and care. Touching diminishes tension. Touching lowers the defense bar. Touching does work wonders when it comes to communicating feelings of love and desire for healing.

4. **Lower Your Voice and Speak Slowly.** Typically, the raised voice and rapid speech are telltale signs that we are out of control — that super-heated emotion is taking over. In those frames of mind, we usually come across as angry, hostile, controlling, but not in charge even of ourselves and our own emotions. A cool, calm low voice sends the message that we are not only in control, but that we have something of significance to offer the stressful situation.

5. **Open the Door.** You may open the door by saying what you wish to say in a positive and non-threatening way. Usually people hear us when we speak in this manner. We need to remember that put-downs, abuse, and badgering will close the heart of the one we are trying to reach more than anything else.

6. **Be empathetic.** Try to understand your partner by putting yourself in his/her shoes. Make a serious attempt to see things from the other's position rather than simply scoring points for

yourself. Try to get inside your partner's mind and heart and experience the issue from his/her perspective. Feel what he/she must be feeling.

7.   **Talk.** Yes, just allow yourself the privilege of talking. Sounds simple enough, but when there is conflict, talk, the one thing that can settle differences, is the last thing couples want to do. The temptation for one or both partners is to "clam up," or "go inside the shell." While it may feel good to go inside the shell and not have to talk, nothing is being resolved and, in fact, the silence is escalating the tension. Remember to use "I Statements" and not "You Statements."

8.   **Take Turns.** When there are differences, they usually exist from both vantage points. No one is 100% right or 100% wrong. No one should have complete command of the conversation. This only deepens the wound and escalates the conflict. Give each other two minute episodes to say what is on the mind and in the heart. Use a stopwatch if necessary. Even the humor of this will break the ice.

9.   **Recognize the Problem.** Don't try to ignore or minimize the problem. Recognize it. Get it on the floor of conversation. Both try to identify and analyze it. Both think of solutions. Try to be specific. Even write out what the problem is and what each thinks is the solution.

10. **Change Locations.** Sometimes conflicts occur in certain settings and once the setting is changed, a new feeling may emerge. Couples may be captives while riding in a car or in a room or in a crowd. Getting away from that location may change the mood of one or both and break down resistance to an open flow of dialogue and mutual exchange of feelings. It is even wise to say, "Why don't we go have a cup of coffee?" Making an appointment to talk allows both people to come to the talking table with a new calmness and expectation. New and intentional environments mean new feelings and new expectations.

11. **Listen to the Heart.** Conflicts develop when feelings have been hurt or egos stepped on. Behind the spoken words are damaged hearts that stand in need of repair. Make a concerted effort not to listen to the words, but to get behind the words to the feelings that are being expressed. Just listening is in itself salve on the wound. Once your loved one has had the time to speak and be heard at the heart, his/her heart is already well on the way toward mending.

12. **Push the Right Buttons.** Couples who have known each other for any amount of time know which buttons to push to make things better or to make them worse. There are sore and sensitive spots which grate on the nerves, spots that draw immediate reflexes and reactions, spots which raise the hackles. It doesn't take a rocket scientist to know where these buttons are once we have known a person for a period of time. But pushing the hot buttons will not only raise the emotional temperature, it will further polarize the relationship. Just as everyone has hot buttons, they also have soft buttons, buttons that when touched have a calming and soothing effect on the one who is touched. Couples also know the soft buttons. Soft buttons are conflict busters for sure!

13. **Say You Care.** Conflict arises when needs are not being met or when wants and desires are at cross-purposes. The underlying message is that the offending party "really doesn't care." One is not concerned about how the other feels. It's "My way or the highway." "He/she never considers what I would like to do." "He and I never seem to be on the same page. He always gets his way!" The conclusion drawn from such statements is that the other doesn't care. Conflict is moderated when there is affirmation that one is truly loved and cared for.

14. **Never Draw a Line of Demarcation.** Drawing a line in the sand is the best way on earth to challenge another. Such lines set limits and draw boundaries, and once drawn, such perimeters are difficult to fracture. Demarcation lines are almost certain to be seen as challenges, and accepting challenges only escalates open verbal warfare. A spirit of openness and desire for communication will erase threats and destroy needs for perimeters.

15. **Communicate Commitment.** Conflict may arise when one member of the partnership feels his/her position is threatened. The most basic of human needs is the need to be loved and the security that goes with the feeling that one is loved. When that security is threatened, gyrations of fear and uncertainty permeate the emotional system. Defenses come into play. The most basic need stands at risk. Conflict emerges. Even when differences are being expressed, and they can be without doing damage the relationship, care should be given to communicate commitment. Such language offers space to explore differences without fear of rejection or alienation.

16. **Be Flexible.** Rigidity or inflexibility are the bugle boys for conflict. When a person is unwilling to bend, he/she is sending the message that it is more important to be right than to mend the brokenness felt in the relationship. Flexibility sends the right message that the one loved is far more important than any rigid position one might hold within oneself. Flexible people are viewed as problem solvers who think and act with sober judgment.

17. **Look for Doors of Opportunity.** The resolution of conflict usually comes with baby steps rather than giant steps. Partners should look for the baby steps, the little nuances which are telltale that the guard is coming down and there is openness to reconciliation. A change of body language, a faint smile, an ever-so-slight alteration of demeanor, a pause in the exchange, subtle suggestions, are all signals that the doors of resolution and reconciliation are opening. Recognizing these baby steps seizes the moment and ultimately leads to the giant steps of resolution and renewal.

18. **Know When to Say When.** If things are not going well, simply call a truce. Put it on a back burner for a while. Even under the best of circumstances and with the best of intentions, things may go south for a spell. Feelings are still raw and nerves frayed. If things are deteriorating and tempers flaring, it may be a good idea to admit that this is not the best time to try to resolve this. Just postpone it until later, but be sure there is a definite time set so that both parties know the conflict has been taken seriously and will be addressed when emotions are more settled.

19. **Write Down the Concern.** If it's important enough to cause conflict, it's important enough to write down. Putting it on paper enables each partner to view the concern more clearly, but also elevates the importance of resolving the issue. Like diagramming a sentence or working a puzzle, getting it out where it can be seen enables each party to get a better view of the whole picture. Putting it on paper also sends up a red flag that this is definitely one of the hot buttons not to push. Once resolved, seldom do couples revisit such sites.

20. **Say You Are Sorry.** Remember that famous quote from *Love Story* when the two young lovers had their first quarrel and an overture is made toward reconciliation. The never-to-be-forgotten response is *"Love means never having to say you are sorry."* While it sounds good in novels and movies, love means being able to say you are sorry and that you do, in fact, want to say it when there has been a breach in the relationship. If there is a balm in Gilead for healing the wounded soul, it is the desire to heal what's broken through a reconciling heart. Dare to repair!!

21. **Don't Rewash Dirty Laundry.** Continuing to focus on issues of the past is usually counterproductive toward resolving conflict. It is important to hear concerns and seek to understand areas that are sensitive, but once they have been addressed, it is best to move on. Dirty laundry is just that: Dirty Laundry, and bringing past issues to the surface will add fuel to the fire and complicate the healing process. Lingering resentment is a sinister force in the arena of putting differences to rest. Couples sometimes need to agree that certain past subjects are simply off limits.

22. **Forgiving Means Forgetting.** When someone has expressed remorse over an issue that caused a conflict, if conflict over the hurt is to be resolved, the injured party must have a forgiving spirit. What is past is past and cannot be redone. An overture for healing the conflict has been extended. Digging at "scabs" will only infect the wound. Once the concern is addressed and the concern is forgiven, it is best to bury it never to be exhumed again.

23. **Be Optimistic!** A firm belief that conflict can be resolved is the launching pad for ultimate restoration. Believing the best about the love of one's life and believing not only that one is loved by that person, but that the loved one also wants resolution will bring results. Pessimism toward resolving differences will only tailspin the healing process. No fissure in relationships is ever mended by believing it can't be resolved. Believing the best brings best results.

24. **Don't Play the Blame Game.** Casting blame will only corner the one with whom one has the conflict. Humans are akin to other species: when cornered, most people tend to strike back. Rather than blaming the other, assuming some responsibility for the breach in the relationship will lower defenses and usually put the conflict on the road to resolution.

25. **Express Gratitude.** The expression of appreciation for the one that is loved can be like magic in the healing process. Gratitude is positive. Gratitude focuses on the good qualities of the one who is loved. Gratitude is remembering the pleasant and not rehashing the offen-

sive. Gratitude enhances rather than diminishes. While gratitude may be difficult when relationships are under stress, the presence of mind to include gratitude in the course of exchange will work wonders.

26. **Be Willing to Give in.** Resistance to reconciliation will only prolong the conflict. If neither partner is willing to give in, there is no opportunity to pour oil on the troubled waters and the stand-off continues, sometimes with even deeper entrenchment. Reconciliation is not about winning and losing. It is about healing and mending what is broken. It is about reaching out to the one that is loved. It involves making oneself vulnerable. A willingness to give in will break the alienation barrier and set the relationship on the course of understanding.

27. **Turn Your Scars into Stars.** The very source of hurt and conflict may prove to be the very place a relationship finds renewal and the capacity to grow again. By processing the conflict, understanding the hurt, reaching for reconciliation, and finding forgiveness and restitution, the downer may prove to be the upper, and an ailing relationship may be restored to health and wholeness where love, trust, and respect are freely given and freely received.

Session V

Notes to the Pastor

This session focuses on the financial aspect of marriage providing couples with necessary support to get their marriage off to a sound beginning with regards to managing their money. The pastor will need to make some judgment calls regarding what needs to be reviewed based on perceived business acumen of the couple. For instance, concerns as simple as keeping a checkbook may be difficult for some couples, while others may consider reviewing such a concern quite elementary.

Points to Be Considered in Session V

- **Tips and strategies for financial solvency**

- **Keeping accurate financial records**

- **Budget "Busters"**

- **Developing and keeping a budget**

- **Reducing debt**

- **Paying interest**

- **Making a will**

Session V

Taking Care of Business

(Helping Couples Plan Ahead)

No pastor wants the couple soon to be married to falter because of the inability to handle themselves financially. Nothing brings stress on a relationship more than not being able to pay the bills or falling further and further behind. Many a couple have started out with every good intention about themselves and their marriage only to discover they were spending more than they were earning and debt was gradually creeping in. The level of income may, in fact, be insignificant as the inability to handle finances may occur to those on the upper, middle, or lower income scale. It is *not* a matter of how much a couple makes; it *is* a matter of being able to budget their lives based on whatever that income level may be.

Once a couple is behind, things may begin to snowball as money is borrowed to remain even current with bills, but borrowed money only complicates the problem as couples find themselves not only paying for what has been borrowed, but the additional interest that continues to accumulate on borrowed funds. Real disaster sets in when funds are borrowed to pay off what has already been borrowed. Couples must understand the need to live within their income and not to get themselves into difficulty through overextending themselves. Once that occurs, there seems to be no end in sight, and tension begins to build. This tension is directed toward the most available target, the one they love and to whom they are married.

Both building a budget and decisions about purchases should be joint decisions. This allows input from both since two heads are better than one, but more importantly, it disallows the blaming game if one makes a financial decision without input or approval from the other. Building a budget together also keeps the financial picture in front of both the husband and the wife as well as impressing upon each to act responsibly and in unity with regards to finance.

Money can simply disappear and no one seems to know where it went. No, no one has taken it. It was in hand once upon a time, but because no one was on top of things, watching where it was going or watching the bottom line, it simply went away. Often when this happens, couples cannot even tell each other where or how the money was spent. This is why records are important. Records give a paper trail as to where funds are going and what proportions of family income are being spent on what causes. Records, even reviewing the Transaction Register in a checkbook, can be very revealing, and at times shocking in terms of what portions of the total income are being spent in areas no one thought possible.

Money management is as important in building and maintaining strong marriages as any other focus. More marriages fall apart not because of lack of income, but simply because couples have not developed the skill to manage what they have. Simply put, *manage your money or it will manage you.* While the pastor does not have the time to train couples in money management, there are several simple tips that may be offered which will point the couple in the right direction, and if followed, will keep them moving their lives forward in terms of financing their lives and future.

84

Concluding the Session

The pastor should summarize what has been shared regarding "Taking Care of Business," again emphasizing the importance of financially managing a marriage and family. Spiritual Journey Inventories should be in the hands of the couple for review of their journey of faith. The pastor may conclude the present session with a prayer reflective of managing a marriage from the perspective of the financial challenges of marriage.

Sample Closing Prayers

Lord, you have called us to be good stewards of what we are given and we are given much. You have reminded us the person who is faithful in little is also faithful in much. As we anticipate the blessings that are ahead, give us a sense of faithfulness in all that you will entrust to our care and keeping. In being faithful, help us never to love any earthly treasure more than we love you. May our faithfulness with our worldly goods be truly reflective of our love for you. Amen.

Everything in heaven and on earth is yours, O Lord. You are the Giver of life and the Giver of all good gifts. In all of our blessings, enable us to be responsible. In the management of our material lives, may we always be guided by your word and Spirit that we may be good and faithful servants. Amen.

You have a plan for us, O God. It is a plan for good and not for evil. Bless these your children, N_____ and N_____, that the plans you have for them may indeed be that solid foundation. May your good plans for them be a contagion for their lives to touch and bless the lives of many. Amen.

Tips and Strategies for Financial Solvency

(Helping Couples Get Ahead and Stay Ahead)

Taking Care of Little Things

Any debt, no matter how small, can be a source of stress and tension if it is unmanageable. There is nothing more distressing than to have even a small debt hanging over your head, if you do not have the funds to pay for it. Receiving statements in the mail or calls from creditors for unpaid debts can bring on unneeded stress or even anxiety attacks. Little debts, debts that would be a pittance to someone financially able, become enormous for someone who is financially strapped. Couples must get in the habit of not spending beyond their means and, at the same time, putting aside a nest egg for the unexpected emergencies that are certain to come. Any couple wishing to build a better mousetrap need only reach for the cheese that lies beyond their grasp to discover the clapper slamming down at a time when they least expect. While this sounds frightening, especially to someone just starting out on their journey of marriage, there is no reason for alarm. Simply planning ahead financially avoids the pitfalls of being caught in the mousetraps where even monetary tidbits seem as giants.

Taking Care of the Books

When couples marry, many decisions have to be made regarding the keeping of the books of the family business. Yes, running a household is a business and should be approached as such. Any business has a cash flow, so much coming in (receipts) and so much going out (debits). Someone must be in charge of keeping an accurate record of the cash flow, making records of it, and being sure that accounts are accurately paid. Selecting the one to do this should be a joint decision of the couple. Two people cannot keep one set of records, as it becomes confusing, and people have different ways of accounting. Logically, the one who is best suited for the job should be the one assigned to do the task. There are any number of assigned tasks in any household, and bookkeeping is only one among several.

Keeping the family books is no small task. Any household will have a considerable amount of money flowing through the bank account. Numerous bills are received on a monthly basis. Besides the usual, such concerns as health insurance, car insurance, income tax, property tax, and school tax may come semi-annually or annually and may come as a jolt to those who have not budgeted ahead for these unusually large sums.

The one whose task it is to keep the books should develop a *system*. Checking out a book from the library on how to keep the books may be helpful in putting the bookkeeping system in place. The system does not have to be complicated, but it does have to be a system and one that works. There are computer programs designed for family bookkeeping, and downloading a simple system will save a lot of energy.

A simple bookkeeping ledger will also do the job. Setting up the system for monthly, quarterly, semi-annual, and annual statements will ensure that nothing is overlooked and ample funds are reserved for the larger statements that do not come on a monthly basis, but nonetheless will appear as payable.

While it should be the task of one person to keep the books, the other should be trained in the system and familiar with when the various bills should be expected. This achieves two ends: 1) It allows the second person to gain perspective on the cost of operating a household, and 2) It prepares that person to do it should the need arise. The business of bookkeeping involves at least two major tasks: Keeping Accurate Financial Records, and Making and Keeping a Budget.

A. Taking Care of Financial Records

Keeping accurate records involves such concerns as keeping the checkbook, keeping records of investments including savings accounts, and monitoring the cash flow.

Account Ownership

Unless there are pre-nuptial agreements or wills stating otherwise, once married, monies by law are commonly owned. Even wills may be contested in a court of law as marriage legally takes preeminence over other legalities in the family law of most states. Most couples want a joint account with both their names on the checkbook and signature card.

Some couples do, however, want to keep their own individual checking accounts so that each has a sense of independence with his or her money. Couples should give this concern careful consideration so that at the outset of the marriage, parameters have been set and each has a clear understanding as to how accounts are to be established and funds expended. The pastor should review this issue with the couple so that it is not left to chance and no surprises arise once the marriage is legally in force. If couples keep separate accounts, decisions must be made regarding who is responsible for what in terms of support for the family. This method of bookkeeping can become very confusing and its fairness may be questioned by either member of the marital dyad. For the purposes of family business, it is much easier to keep one set of books, and simply have an understanding regarding spending limits for the husband and the wife.

Checking Account

The checking account is basic to family bookkeeping. Some people only have a vague idea as to what is in their checking account and, in fact, depend on the bank to keep their records. Some do not understand that the bank statement does not reflect the actual amount in the account, only the amount, according to bank records, when the statement was summarized and mailed.

Bank statements will provide several types of important information that should be carefully reviewed upon arrival. The **account summary** will provide the **previous balance** with the date of the last summary, the number of **deposits/credits,** the number of **checks/debits,** and the **service charge.** The initial step for the one keeping the checkbook is to verify that the **account summary** corresponds to the record contained within the checkbook. The following section on the bank statement will be an accounting of **checks paid.** Check transactions will be provided according to the sequential number that is found in the upper right hand corner of the check. The date of the transaction, not the date of the check, the amount of the check, and the reference number are also provided in the information section for checks paid.

The third section of the statement is an accounting of **deposits and other credits.** The transaction record will include: the date of the deposit, the amount, and the description of the transaction as to whether it is a deposit or other credit such as interest paid on the account, along with the reference number.

Finally, the statement will provide a **daily balance summary.** This part of the statement gives the date and the balance in the account based on deposits and credits and debits from checks written. The final balance here should correspond to the new balance for the account. A cross examination of all these four transaction records will ensure that the account is balanced (also called reconciled) between the record of the bank and the transaction register in the checkbook.

Transaction Register

The Transaction Register provides space for recording a number of items referencing each transaction. These include the check number, the date, the transaction description, the payment/debit, the code for the payment, the fee, the deposit/credit, and the balance. Below is a sample of a Transaction Register.

Transaction Register

Number	Date	Transaction Description	Payment/ Debit	Code	Fee	Deposit/ Credit	Balance	
101	2/5	Home Life Ins Co.	231.15				$1339	15
102	2/8	Publix Grocery Store	113.87				1225	45
	2/10	Cash Withdrawn	50.00	ATM	.50		1174	95
103	2/10	Deposit Dan's Check		D		631.90	1806	85
	2/11	American Mortgage	831.88	AP			974	97
	2/12	Duke Power Co.	156.76				818	21

Code for Non-Check Transactions
- **D** Deposit
- **DP** Debit Credit Purchase
- **ATM** Cash Withdrawal
- **AP** Automatic Payment
- **I** Interest Earned
- **SC** Service Charge

Balancing an Account

When the bank sends the bank statement, it is important to reconcile the checkbook with the bank statement. This may be accomplished by comparing each section of the statement with the checkbook Transaction Register, first by comparing the account summary of the bank with that in the checkbook. This ensures that the number of deposits, number of checks, and amount of the service charge, as reported by the bank, correspond to the record in the checkbook. The following steps will ensure that an accurate record for the account balance is correct.

1. Transaction Register items such as preauthorized drafts, service charges, interest credits, and automatic transfers that have not been recorded in the checkbook Transaction Register should be recorded.

2. In the Transaction Register all checks and debits/withdrawals as shown on the bank statement should be marked off.

3. Any transaction not accounted for in the statement should be accounted for.
   A. Outstanding Checks/Debits which do not appear in the statement.
   B. Deposits/Credits not accounted for in the statement.

4. Write the statement ending balance shown on the bank statement. $_____

5. Add the amount of outstanding Deposits/Credits from Step 3 B. $_____

6. Total lines 4 and 5. $_____

7. Subtract the amount of outstanding Checks/Debits from Step 3 A. $_____

8. This is the adjusted balance. This balance should agree with the current register balance.

$_____

If the adjusted statement balance does not agree with the transaction register balance, one might review last month's reconcilement to make sure any differences were corrected as well as making sure all deposits shown on the statement are included in the register balance. If there are inconsistencies between the two, the Bank Customer Representative should be contacted.

B. Developing and Maintaining a Budget

It is important that any couple keep a budget that accurately reflects their income and expenditures. Below is a chart that may assist couples in developing an annual budget based on monthly income.

Monthly Income	
Income from Husband after Withholdings:	$_____
Income from Wife after Withholdings:	$_____
Commissions:	$_____
Bonuses:	$_____
Investment Income (Interest, Rentals, etc.)	$_____
Other Income:	$_____
Total Monthly Income:	$_____
Multiply by 12 for Annual Income:	$_____

The monthly income should be multiplied by twelve, adding any other unreported yearly income to the bottom line to determine the true annual income. The annual income provides the basis for developing a budget that reflects both income and cost of operating a household based on valid, realistic figures.

Budget preparation begins with the development of an annual budget simply because there are costs which are annual costs that may not be apparent on a monthly basis. All the cost of operating a household should be collectively summed to arrive at one inclusive figure. That total figure represents every category needful for the operation of the family unit. These categories include: housing, food, debts, contributions, car/transportation costs, insurance, recreation/leisure, clothing, medical expenses, savings/investments, day care/school costs, and miscellaneous expenses. An annual budget reflective of these categories will indicate how much it costs to operate the household based on each particular category, i.e., cost of housing, cost of food, etc.

A monthly budget may be prepared based on the figures of the annual budget. The monthly budget should now include costs that may be annual or semi-annual, but nonetheless, must be accounted for and included as costs of operating the household on a monthly basis. These may include such costs as car insurance or property taxes that are not usually billed on a monthly basis. The following table may serve to enable a couple to build an annual budget.

Annual Family Budget

Housing

Mortgage (Including
Principle, Interest,
Taxes, and Insurance) _____

Rent _____

Utilities (Electricity,
Phone, Water, Gas,
Cable) _____

Upkeep of Property _____

Other Housing
Expenses _____

Total Housing Cost $_____

Food

Cost of Groceries and
related expenses _____

Total Food Cost $_____

Recreation & Leisure

Leisure Activities (sports,
dining out) _____

Vacations _____

Related Costs to Above _____

Total Rec. & Leisure $_____

Contributions

Church _____

Charities _____

Total Contributions $_____

Clothing

Total Clothing Cost $_____

Medical Expenses

Physicians _____

Dentists _____

Prescriptions _____

Total Medical $_____

Car and Transportation

Payments for car /
car rental _____

Upkeep of car (gas,
repair, maintenance) _____

Related car expenses
(tags, insurance, parking) _____

Taxis or subway _____

Total Transportation $_____

Insurance

Medical _____

Dental _____

Life _____

Other _____

Total Insurance $_____

Debt Retirement

Loans _____

Credit Cards _____

Total Debt Retirement $_____

Savings & Investments

Total Savings & Invest. $_____

School & Day Care

Total School & Day Care $_____

Miscellaneous

Total Miscellaneous $_____

Total Cost of Living $_____

Income $_____

**Difference
(Plus or Minus)** $_____

The ***Annual Family Budget*** table is based on annual income and expenditures. Dividing the annual budget by twelve will provide an understandable picture of how monies are being spent on a monthly basis. A monthly budget will analyze the spending data in much greater detail. Computing the monthly figures for quarterly or semi-annual totals will give a "heads up" on where a couple may stand with regards to income versus expenditures.

When the **Total Cost of Living** is subtracted from **Family Income**, there will either be a surplus or a deficit. Unfortunately, when couples are just beginning the budgeting process, there is usually a deficit as unexpected expenses crop up that are not figured into the budget. This means that the budget has to be "tweaked" in order to adjust in areas that are out of balance. Reviewing the budget may also reveal areas of spending that were not included in the original budget and adjustments have to made in order to make the budget realistic. Both the income and spending categories must be examined and spending must be adjusted unless there is some way to create a greater income.

At the outset of a marriage, it is most important that couples not outspend their income. Therefore, it is advisable to encourage them to make difficult spending decisions. In order to keep the spending even with the income, some sacrifices may have to be made, but sacrifices made early will strengthen financial conditions later on.

C. Taking Care of the Business of Reducing Debt

It is easy for a couple to accumulate a sizable debt without realizing the debt is mounting, and debts that are not met head-on can sabotage the financial health of a family. Newly-married couples may have residual expenses associated with the wedding or debts acquired previous to the marriage. Persons may bring such debts as college loans, car loans, or even debts acquired in previous relationships, into the marriage. Bringing outstanding debts into a relationship must be addressed up front so that both parties are cognizant of their existence and nothing is hidden from view only to surface after the "knot is tied." It is a matter of honesty that each partner disclose any debt that is outstanding and the pastor should put this on the agenda of conversation. How might one feel to be married only to discover that the act of marriage put him/her in financial straits?

In order that debts not seriously damage the financial well-being of a couple, a plan of action must be put into place to reduce and/or eradicate the outstanding balances. If there are multiple debts, the entire list must be computed both in order to get a true picture of all that is owed and to develop a plan for repayment. Most debts are on a monthly payment plan and if there are no overdue debts, the payment plan for debt reduction may simply fit into the planned family budget. Any debts that are past due should be paid first so that a couple's credit remains in good standing. It is also a good idea to try to reduce small debts first simply to reduce the number and make repayment more manageable. This allows a couple to move on to focus on the larger debts and reduces the anxiety of multiple debts. If the repayment of debt becomes a problem, professional guidance should be sought. Any community has a number of financial counselors who will assist couples in developing a plan to resolve their financial problems. Most lending institutions also provide assistance and guidance, as it is in their best interest to provide repayment plans, and most will work with anyone when it is evident there is honest intent to repay. Most lending agencies will go the extra mile to be a resource for help, but the borrower must first make it known that help is needed.

A simple call and appointment will usually set up the groundwork for developing a plan from the lending institution.

D. Taking Care of the Business of Paying Interest

The amount of interest any couple may pay in a lifetime can be astounding. Interest comes in several forms and at different rates. When anything is purchased on time, there is the carrying charge of interest, so couples need to be aware that interest is also money and must be figured into the total cost of the purchase.

Most sellers would like to sell their commodities on time because profit is received not only from the sale of the product, but also from the interest paid. In this case, interest is also a commodity, as it has not only become part of the purchase price, but an entity within itself. The most common forms of interest facing couples include Interest on the Mortgage, Interest on Big Ticket Items such as automobiles or appliances, and Credit Card Interest.

Credit Cards

Credit card interest is usually the highest form of interest, ranging from 18 to 21%. Since money is a commodity, banks want clients to use credit cards. Unpaid monthly balances bring banks huge profits from credit card debts, and such an ongoing practice can put a couple at risk, as it can reach a point in which interest is being paid on interest. Plastic money has become the way of doing business, but care must be given that such credit does not quickly get out of hand. Credit cards are convenient and may even serve as paper trails for spending. However, payment of the credit card balance as soon as it arrives will avoid the high interest commensurate with unpaid balances on plastic money.

Mortgage Loans

Mortgage rates rise and fall based on the prime interest rate as set by the federal lending institutions. While home ownership can be a great investment, given the appreciation of most properties, care should be given to acquire the best mortgage rate possible, not simply settling for what is convenient. Mortgage rates, like any other commodity, are competitive, and some simple legwork may save a couple thousands of dollars as just a percentage point's difference in the rate can mean huge sums when amortized over a number of years. Homebuyers should go shopping for the best rate and lending institutions may also "bargain" to get the business.

Mortgage rates also fluctuate according to changes in the Treasury Bill rates. Interest-rate movements are based on supply and demand. If there are more buyers, sellers can get a better price (Sellers' Market), but higher rates. If the demand for credit reduces (Buyers' Market), so do interest rates. When the economy is growing, there is a higher demand for credit, so rates go up. If the economy is slowing, the demand for credit goes down and so do interest rates. The bad news is that a slowing economy is good news for lower interest rates and the good news is that a growing economy is bad news for the interest rates in that they will be higher.

The driving force of interest rates is inflation. Higher inflation means a growing economy. When the economy is growing too quickly, the Federal Reserve increases interest rates to slow down the economy and reduce inflation. A strong economy results in higher prices for goods and services, real estate, and higher mortgage rates. Mortgage rates usually move in the same direction as interest rates.

If mortgage rates appear to be going down, waiting a few days to apply for and process a loan may also be a source of saving huge sums for the home buyer over a period of time. Conversely, if mortgage rates are going up, the sooner the loan is processed, the better for the buyer.

Mortgage rates are published in some newspapers and may be reviewed on a comparative basis. Calling lending institutions and simply asking what their present mortgage rate is will also provide the needed information. A good mortgage company that has the client's interest in mind may be the best place to find the best rate. One should keep in mind that lending institutions may vary as much as one to two percentage points on their rates. One point's difference when paid over a thirty-year period represents a sizable amount of money.

The principle of amortization is that the lending institution puts the weight of the interest on the front end of the repayment schedule. For example, on examining a 7% thirty-year loan, one will discover that the first month's payment of $997.95 will see only $122.95 going toward the principle and $875.00 going toward interest. During the course of the thirty years, the amount going toward the interest goes down while the amount going toward the principle goes up so that on the last payment, number 360, $992.18 goes toward principle and $5.78 goes toward interest. Only on payment 242 does the amount going to principle exceed the amount going to interest.

In the course of buying a house that cost $150,000 in the example cited, the buyer will pay a total of $359,263 that represents $209,263.00 paid out in interest. While these figures are startling, buying a house is still a good investment in an appreciating market as people nowadays are mobile and are looking for appreciated equity in one house in order to upgrade themselves on the next purchase.

Car Payments

Car payments are also amortized so that the interest is weighted toward the front of the loan. A car that cost $20,000.00 with a 7% loan paid over a period of five years will accrue a total of $3,761.44 in interest. The first month's payment of $396.02 will see $116.67 going toward interest and only $279.36 going toward the principle. On the sixtieth and last payment, only $2.30 goes toward interest and $393.72 goes toward the principle. Almost 19% of the cost of the car has gone toward interest on a 7% five-year loan.[1]

E. Taking Care of the Business of Making a Will

The importance of a will cannot be overstated, and it is incumbent on the pastor to impress upon the couple the importance of having a will prepared. Most couples do not consider the importance of a will at the outset of marriage, thinking that this is something that can be put on a back burner until a later time. Young couples are especially prone not to think about a will, as drawing up a will seems to be an item that can wait until much later in life. People may spend a lifetime accumulating assets and never take the few hours required to determine what is going to happen to those assets in the event they are not around. It is quite alarming that 70% of people die without a will.

There are several reasons a will is of utmost importance. Here are but a few:

1. Everyone has assets and most people have more assets than they imagine. Failure to make provision for what will happen to those assets will leave the distribution of those assets in the hands of the state who will follow state laws and proceedings regarding distributions. Such distributions may not be in keeping with the wishes of the decedent.

2. Dying without a will may create burdensome court proceedings, not to mention the added legal expenses. Such cases may extend settlements into the future for unbelievable extended periods of time.

3. In some instances of death without a will, children may become the ward of the state and a state-appointed guardian may be utilized in the rearing of children. The appointee may be unknown to the family and rear children apart from the values or goals of the deceased parents.

4. In some cases, the absence of a will at the time of death subjugates the estate to higher taxes than may have otherwise been had careful provision and planning been made prior to death.

5. Wills expedite proceedings and ensure that the wishes of the deceased are fulfilled. People postpone the making of wills for various reasons, procrastination and expense being two of those. For the obvious reasons cited, couples should take care of making a will at their earliest convenience. The expense of making a will is negligible in terms of what it may cost the estate later on. In fact, the cost of a will may be nothing more than the time to do it. Doing a will is as simple as obtaining a sample copy from the library or off the internet and customizing it to the particular needs and wishes of the person/couple, and having it properly notarized. Sample copies of wills may be found in the addendum of this publication.

Session VI

Notes to the Pastor

Couples who seek out a pastor and church setting for their wedding usually do so because theirs is a faith-based life, having both grown up in the church and having some measure of commitment to the values and teaching of the Christian faith. In all probability, they have shared some of their faith with one another either by attending worship together or in open conversation. This session is an opportunity for the couple to discuss formally their faith either privately, or in the presence of the pastor. Couples may have privately wished to discuss their faith, but have never had the forum in which to do so.

Points to Be Considered in Session VI

- **The Spiritual Journeys of the Bride and Groom**

- **Meanings of Scripture Passages**

- **People Who Were Influential in their Spiritual Journey**

Session VI

Faith in the Context of Marriage

Couples who wish to be married by a pastor in a church do so for a reason, not just for the aesthetics of a church wedding. They could be married in a secular setting without the benefit of the clergy or any representation of Christian faith. Their coming to the pastor sends a strong message that they want their marriage not simply to be legally recognized by the state, but blessed by the church. Thus, from the perspective of the pastor, a door has been opened to explore and even deepen their journey of faith. This setting has placed the pastor in a unique position for open dialogue with the couple about their faith and their relationship with God and their walk with Christ. The approach the pastor uses will determine the success for open and honest sharing. By now the couple feels comfortable talking with the pastor, but invading the heart and soul of one's faith is a bit more personal. Care must be given to allow the couple to share their faith journey openly and honestly and without fear of judgment.

During the course of ministry, pastors will meet with couples who share a wide range of religious perspective and experience, from those whose journey has been a close personal walk to those for whom faith is objective and distant. Partners in the relationship may be at different stages in their journey. One may have grown up in the church and never known anything other than a deep personal faith, while for the other, even talk about personal faith is a new experience. One may be privately attempting to move the other along toward a more genuine faith experience. Both may be members of the church "in name only," or both may share a very personal faith at the deepest level.

The fact that the couple is sitting before the pastor who represents the church is a stepping-stone to opening the conversation about spiritual journeys and the Christian context of marriage. The pastor may open the session by observing the couple has come to the church for solemnization of their wedding vows rather than elsewhere. The pastor may then go on to explain there is a different understanding of marriage from the perspective of the church and the perspective of the state. The state sees marriage as a binding legal or social contract, while the church understands marriage as a covenant made under God and in the presence of fellow members of the Christian family. Such a pledge endures, not because of the force of law or fear of its actions, but because an unconditional covenant has been made. It is a covenant more solemn, more binding, and more permanent than any legal contract.

Indeed, the Christian context of marriage has been defined as "a relationship between a man and a woman intended by God to be a monogamous relationship, intended to be a permanent bond in which many needs are satisfied — the need to love and be loved, the need for deep friendship, for sharing, for companionship, for children, the need to escape loneliness. Marriage ought to be a bond of love, reflecting the love Christ has for his people, a bond of sacrificial love where husband and wife have become one, one flesh, one unity."[2] Even though the couple has chosen to be married in the church by a pastor, they may not clearly understand the difference between the Christian covenantal and the secular base. The first task for the pastor is to distinguish between the two. Read aloud the two definitions of Christian marriage above with the following questions:

1. How is the Christian understanding of marriage different from simply a legal or social contract?

2. What is a covenant?

3. From the perspective of the church, before whom is the covenant made?

4. Why would a Christian covenant be more lasting than simply a legal contract?

5. How would the love of Christ be reflected in the sacrificial bond of love a husband and wife have for each other?

Having laid groundwork for open sharing regarding the couple's faith journey, the pastor may now move on to review the **Spiritual Journey Inventory** that the couple has filled out and has in hand.

Concluding the Session

The pastor may conclude the session with a prayer reflective of the faith journeys that have been shared and discussed. The couple should be reminded that the next task in the interview process is to review the actual wedding service itself.

Sample Closing Prayers

Lord, as we reflect on our spiritual journeys, we have come to understand yet again what an important person you are in our lives and in our relationship. We thank you for parents who set our feet toward your house and instilled a deep love for you within our hearts. We thank you for the communities of faith of which we have been so privileged to have been a part. We remember with thanksgiving those important spiritual leaders in our lives, the Sunday School teachers, the pastors, the mentors, and those who so willingly gave of themselves that we may have a fuller knowledge of you and a closer walk of faith. As we think of the home that is to be our home, may the faith given us be a blessing and an integral part of each and every day. Amen.

God of grace and glory, how magnificent is your name in all the earth. In reflecting upon our separate journeys with you, and now anticipating the day when we two shall become as one, we are truly reminded that you are a God who is working out your purposes and sharing your presence in the lives of your children. How grateful we are to have found another who shares our Christian faith. We know your hand has been in the love we have found in one another. Holy God, bless N_____ and N_____ in their spiritual journey and be the unseen, yet ever present guest in the home they will establish. Amen.

We are reminded that where two or three are gathered together, there are you among them, O Lord. Our time today enables us to know that N_____ and N_____ have come together in your name and presence and we have felt that presence as we have shared. Go with this couple. Always be in their midst. May their faith keep growing and growing and may they find every grace and peace in your presence and love. Amen.

Groom's Spiritual Journey Inventory

1. Write a brief description of your journey of faith. You may describe how you came to know and understand God, important people who led you to faith, experiences you have had along the way, or some turning point in your life that led you to faith.

_____

_____

_____

_____

_____

_____

2. Who is God and how has God played an important part of your life? _____

_____

_____

_____

_____

3. In Genesis 2:18-25 we read:

Then the Lord God said, "It is not good that the man should be alone; I will make a helper for him." So out of the ground the Lord God formed every beast of the field and bird of the air, and brought them to the man to see what he would call them; and whatever the man called every living creature, that was its name. The man gave names to all cattle, and to the birds of the air, and to every beast of the field; but for the man there was not found a helper fit for him. So the Lord God caused a deep sleep to fall upon the man, and while he slept took one of his ribs and closed up its place with flesh; and the rib which the Lord God had taken from the man he made into a woman and brought her to the man. Then the man said,

"This at last is bone from my bones
and flesh from my flesh;
This shall be called Woman,
because she was taken out of the man."

Therefore a man leaves his father and his mother and cleaves to his wife and they become one flesh.

Reflecting on this passage,

A. How would you relate this passage to your upcoming marriage? _____

_____

_____

_____

B. From the passage, what purposes does God have for marriage? _____

_____

_____

_____

C. What is meant by the term "helper"? How might you and your wife-to-be prove to be helpers for one another?

_____

_____

_____

D. What is implied by the term to "leave one's father and mother"? _____

_____

_____

_____

4. The Song of Solomon 8:6-7 says:

> *Set me as a seal upon your heart,*
> *as a seal upon your arm;*
> *for love is strong as death,*
> *and jealousy cruel as the grave.*
> *Its flashes are flashes of fire,*
> *a most vehement flame.*
> *Many waters cannot quench love,*
> *neither can floods drown it.*
> *If a man offered for love*
> *all the wealth of his house*
> *it would be utterly scorned.*

A. What important thought is Solomon sharing with these words? _____

_____

_____

_____

B. What images of love in your relationship may be reflected in this passage? _____

_____

_____

_____

5. Below is a list of scripture lessons that pertain to faith and love and which may be applied to marriage. Review the list and select two passages that particularly speak to you and upon which you would like to base your marriage.

Old Testament:

Ruth 1:16-17
Psalm 67:1-3
Psalm 100
Psalm 103
Psalm 117
Psalm 121
Proverbs 31:10-31
Hosea 2:16-20

New Testament:

Matthew 5:13-16
Matthew 7:24-28
Matthew 19:3-6
John 2:1-11
John 15:9-17
Romans 8:31-39
Romans 12:9-21
I Corinthians 13
Ephesians 3:14-21
Ephesians 5:2, 21-33
Colossians 3:12-17
I Peter 3:1-7
I John 4:7-16

A. _____ First Passage Selected

Why did you select this passage and how might its content be applied to your marriage?

_____

_____

_____

_____

B. _____ Second Passage Selected

How does this passage reflect your spiritual journey? What in this passage may be your spiritual foundation for marriage?

_____

_____

_____

_____

6. In Mark 10:6-9, Jesus says:

"But from the beginning of creation,
'God made them male and female.'
'For this reason a man shall leave his
father and mother and be joined to his wife,
And the two shall become one.'
So they are no longer two but one.
What therefore God has joined together,
let no man put asunder."

The theme of this passage is that two people, when they are married, become as one. What are some ways that you may seek and uphold a sense of oneness in your marriage?

_____

_____

_____

_____

_____

7. Do you feel comfortable talking to your wife-to-be about your spiritual journey? _____

_____

8. Were your parents religious? _____ Did they take you to Sunday School and church?

_____

9. In terms of your Christian journey, who influenced you the most in life? _____

_____

Bride's Spiritual Journey Inventory

1. Write a brief description of your journey of faith. You may describe how you came to know and understand God, important people who led you to faith, experiences you have had along the way, or some turning point in your life that led you to faith.

_____

_____

_____

_____

_____

_____

2. Who is God and how has God played an important part of your life? _____

_____

_____

_____

_____

_____

3. In Genesis 2:18-25 we read:

*Then the Lord God said, "It is not good that the man should be alone; I will make a helper for him."
So out of the ground the Lord God formed every beast of the field and bird of the air, and brought
them to the man to see what he would call them; and whatever the man called every living creature,
that was its name. The man gave names to all cattle, and to the birds of the air, and to every beast
of the field; but for the man there was not found a helper fit for him. So the Lord God caused a deep
sleep to fall upon the man, and while he slept took one of his ribs and closed up its place with flesh;
and the rib which the Lord God had taken from the man he made into a woman and brought her to
the man. Then the man said,*

"This at last is bone from my bones
and flesh from my flesh;
This shall be called Woman,
because she was taken out of the man."

Therefore a man leaves his father and his mother and cleaves to his wife and they become one flesh.

Reflecting on this passage,

A. How would you relate this passage to your upcoming marriage? _____

_____

_____

_____

B. From the passage, what purposes does God have for marriage? _____

_____

_____

_____

C. What is meant by the term "helper"? How might you and your husband-to-be prove to be helpers for one another?

_____

_____

_____

D. What is implied by the term to "leave one's father and mother"? _____

_____

_____

_____

4. The Song of Solomon 8:6-7 says:

Set me as a seal upon your heart,
as a seal upon your arm;
for love is strong as death,
and jealousy cruel as the grave.
Its flashes are flashes of fire,
a most vehement flame.
Many waters cannot quench love,
neither can floods drown it.
If a man offered for love
all the wealth of his house
it would be utterly scorned.

What images of love in your relationship may be reflected in this passage? _____

_____

_____

_____

5. Below is a list of scripture lessons that pertain to faith and love and which may be applied to marriage. Review the list and select two passages that particularly speak to you and upon which you would like to base your marriage.

Old Testament:

Ruth 1:16-17
Psalm 67:1-3
Psalm 100
Psalm 103
Psalm 117
Psalm 121
Proverbs 31:10-31
Hosea 2:16-20

New Testament:

Matthew 5:13-16
Matthew 7:24-28
Matthew 19:3-6
John 2:1-11

108

John 15:9-17
Romans 8:31-39
Romans 12:9-21
I Corinthians 13
Ephesians 3:14-21
Ephesians 5:2, 21-33
Colossians 3:12-17
I Peter 3:1-7
I John 4:7-16

A. _____ First Passage Selected

Why did you select this passage and how might its content be applied to your marriage?

_____

_____

_____

_____

B. _____ Second Passage Selected

How does this passage reflect your spiritual journey? What in this passage may be your spiritual foundation for marriage?

_____

_____

_____

_____

6. In Mark 10:6-9, Jesus says:

> *"But from the beginning of creation,*
> *'God made them male and female.'*
> *'For this reason a man shall leave his*
> *father and mother and be joined to his wife,*
> *And the two shall become one.'*

So they are no longer two but one.
What therefore God has joined together,
let no man put asunder."

The theme of this passage is that two people, when they are married, become as one. What are some ways that you may seek and uphold a sense of oneness in your marriage?

_____

_____

_____

_____

_____

_____

7. Do you feel comfortable talking to your husband-to-be about your spiritual journey? _____

_____

9. Were your parents religious? _____ Did they take you to Sunday School and church?

_____

10. In terms of your Christian journey, who influenced you the most in life? _____

_____

Session VII

Notes to the Pastor

Reviewing the wedding service itself, including the rubrics, is one of the more important tasks of premarital counseling. Session VII walks the couple through the wedding service using the support of sample services from four major Protestant denominations that serve as examples of any typical service. Focus points are provided for the support of the pastor in delineating the meanings of the vows in order that couples have an understanding of the promises they are making in the marriage covenant.

Points to Be Considered in Session VII

- **The ceremony is central to the entire wedding celebration**

- **Marriage vows from four typical services**

- **Focus points reflecting the meaning of the wedding service**

- **Appropriate wedding scriptures**

Session VII

Reviewing the Marriage Service

(Enabling Couples to Understand Their Wedding Vows)

Often couples go through the entire process of planning their wedding, including every aspect of every event that surrounds the wedding, and yet are never given the opportunity to review the service with the pastor with explanations of what particular parts of the ceremony may mean. Since the ceremony itself is the most important part of the wedding celebration, it is important that the pastor sit down with the bride and groom and carefully review each component of the service, giving the couple ample explanation for the content of the service.

Pastors from various denominations and communions usually use their own denomination's book of worship and liturgy for the service, although there are a number of services available and couples may, in fact, write their own vows. However, most services generally follow the same order and vows expressed have similarity in the promises made. Regardless of what form the service may take, huge commitments are being made and the pastor should carefully review those commitments with the couple in order that they understand the promises they are making.

Following are several orders of service that represent various communions and denominations. While these are by no means inclusive orders of services, they are representative of a broad range of ceremonies. Pastors should correlate the services and commentary included here with their own denomination's services or the service they use for wedding ceremonies. The services are **coded** as follows:

Baptist:	**B**
Presbyterian:	**P**
United Methodist:	**UM**
United Church of Christ:	**UCC**

B: Prelude
Processional
Call to Worship
Affirmation of Marriage
Exchange of Vows
Scripture Lesson
Exchange of Rings
Pronouncement of Marriage
Communion Service (if celebrated)
Blessing and Presentation
Recessional

P: Prelude
Processional and Entrance
Statement of the Gift of Marriage
Prayer
Declaration of Intent
Affirmation of the Families
Affirmation of the Congregation
Readings from the Scriptures
Sermon
Vows
Exchange of Rings
Prayer
Lord's Prayer
Announcement of Marriage
Charge and Blessing
Recessional

UM: Gathering
Greeting
Declaration of Intention
Response of the Families
Prayer
Proclamation and Response
Sermon or Witness to Christian Marriage
Exchange of Vows
Blessing and Exchange of Rings
Declaration of Marriage
Blessing of the Marriage
Thanksgiving and Communion (if celebrated)
Lord's Prayer
Dismissal and Blessing
The Peace
Going Forth

UCC: Prelude
Processional and Entrance
Greeting
Introduction
Prayer
Reading of Scripture
Sermon
Declaration of Intention
Pledge of Support
Vows of the Marriage Covenant

Exchange of Symbols
Announcement of Marriage
Blessing
Prayer of Our Savior
Holy Communion (if celebrated)
Benediction
Recessional
Postlude

PRELUDE OR GATHERING

The prelude is a time for the seating of the guests for the wedding. Usually the groomsmen will seat the guests according to whether they are guests of the bride or guests of the groom, with the bride's guests seated on the left facing the chancel and the groom's guests seated on the right facing the chancel. Special seating is reserved for special guests including parents, grandparents, and others whom the couple wish to honor with reserved seating. Special guests are the last to be seated and should be seated in reverse order of how they shall be escorted out of the church. That is, special guests are seated first, grandparents, then parents of the groom, and lastly the mother of the bride. Prelude music should be carefully chosen in coordination with the music director. The prelude is a time for guests to *reflect* and *meditate* on the meaning of marriage and the couple whose marriage they are honoring by their presence.

PROCESSIONAL OR ENTRANCE

The processional is the time for those in the wedding party to enter the sanctuary. The couple to be married may enter together or separately, depending on local traditions and preferences of the couple. Usually the groom and best man enter with the pastor and are the first members of the wedding party to take their places within the chancel setting. Groomsmen enter either walking in single file or as twosomes. Groomsmen may also process in by escorting the bridesmaids. Bridesmaids follow the groomsmen, usually in single file. The maid or matron of honor will follow the bridesmaids, followed by the ring bearer and flower girl. A change in the music tempo, volume, or musical selection, in addition to closing and re-opening the sanctuary doors the bride and her escort are to enter, will give a heightened effect to the joy of the moment that "something grand and wonderful" is about to take place, and that this is "the bride's moment." Also, all guests should stand upon her entrance. The standing is best signaled as the bride's mother stands in honor of her daughter.

The processional may engage forms of celebration such as banners, ribbons, white carpet runners, etc., in accordance with local custom. A hymn, canticle, anthem, or instrumental music may also be played to accentuate the joyful worship and celebrative mood of the moment.

THE GREETING OR WELCOME

Normally, the pastor begins the service with a greeting that is usually a scripture verse, although a personal statement of greeting will also serve to begin the celebration.

Scriptural greetings may include:

P: Pastor: "God is love, and those who abide in love,
abide in God." I John 4:16

Or

P: Pastor: "This is the day that the Lord has made;
let us rejoice and be glad in it." Psalm 118: 24[3]

Or

UCC: Pastor: "The grace of our Lord Jesus Christ
and the love of God and the communion of the
Holy Spirit be with you all." II Corinthians 13:14

Or

UCC: Pastor: "Love comes from God.
Everyone who truly loves is a child of God." I John 4:7
Let us worship God.[4]

Pastoral Greetings without the use of scripture may include:

B: Pastor: When Jesus was invited to the marriage at Cana of
Galilee, he gladly joined the happy company and there began
his ministry and acts of power. Since that day the
entrance of Christ into homes which bid him welcome has
been the occasion of great joy, rich blessing, and spiritual growth.
Desiring his companionship at the beginning of their wedded
life, N_____ and N_____ have called us to be witnesses
before our Lord of the pledges they are about to make to each other,
and to set them forth in their new estate by our prayers and Christian
greetings.[5]

UM: Pastor: Friends, we are gathered together in the sight of God
to witness and bless the joining together of N_____ and N_____
in Christian marriage.

The covenant of marriage was established by God,
who created us male and female for each other
with his presence and power.
Jesus graced a wedding at Cana of Galilee,
and in his sacrificial love
gave us the example for the love of husband and wife.
N_____ and N _____ come to give themselves to one another
in this holy covenant.[6]

Focus Points the Pastor May Review with the Couple

1. The wedding is a worship service. While it is a special service within the context of worship in the church, it is nonetheless a service of worship. The calls to worship, whether scriptural or written affirmation, affirm the spiritual nature of the service as each focuses on the faith-based nature of the service and of marriage itself.

2. The service is an affirmation of our faith in Christ. While the service joins the wedding couple in marriage, the underlying theme of the service is the presence of Christ in marriage, whether at Cana or the present service.

3. There is a great sense of joy in a wedding celebration. The joy is expressed in the scriptural passages and in the written calls to worship. Couples should understand that God is the giver of joy in every good gift, including their marriage.

INTRODUCTION/STATEMENT ON MARRIAGE

B: Pastor: The rite of marriage in which you are now come is the first and oldest rite of mankind. This most blessed and lasting of human relationships was first celebrated in the bowers of Eden in the time when man was innocent. God saw that it was not good for the man to live alone so he created woman to be man's companion and wife. Marriage was given to us in the wisdom of God to soothe the troubles and increase the joys of this earthly life. This is God's will for you, if you purpose in your hearts to beautify and sweeten it by your tender devotion for one another, your mindfulness in little things, and your patience and sacrifice to self and each other. Coming in full love to the threshold of a new life together, I ask you to join hands.

P: Pastor: We gather in the presence of God
to give thanks for the gift of marriage,
to witness the joining of N_____ and N_____,
to surround them with our prayers,
and to ask God's blessing upon them,
so that they may be strengthened for their life together
and nurtured in their love for God.

God created us male and female,
and gave us marriage
so that husband and wife may help and comfort each other,
living faithfully together in plenty and in want,
in joy and in sorrow,
in sickness and in health,
throughout all their days.

God gave us marriage
for the full expression of the love between a man and a woman.
In marriage a woman and a man belong to each other,
and with affection and tenderness
freely give themselves to each other.

God gave us marriage
for the well-being of human society,
for the ordering of family life,
and for the birth and nurture of children.

God gave us marriage as a holy mystery
in which a man and a woman are joined together,
and become one,
just as Christ is one with the church.

In marriage, husband and wife are called to a new way of life,
created, ordered, and blessed by God.
This way of life must not be entered into carelessly,
or from selfish motives,
but responsibly, and prayerfully.

We rejoice that marriage is given by God,
blessed by our Lord Jesus Christ,
and sustained by the Holy Spirit.
Therefore, let marriage be held in honor by all.

UCC: Pastor: Dear friends,
we have come together
in the presence of God
to witness the marriage
of N_____
and N_____
to surround them
with our prayers,
and to share
in their joy.

The scriptures teach us
that the bond and covenant
of marriage is a gift of God,
holy mystery
in which a man and woman
become one flesh,
an image of the union
of Christ and the church.

As this woman and this man
give themselves to each other today,
we remember that at Cana in Galilee
our Savior Jesus Christ
made the wedding feast
a sign of God's reign of love.

Let us enter this celebration
confident that through the Holy Spirit
Christ is present with us now.
We pray that this couple may
fulfill God's purpose for the
whole of their lives.

Focus Points the Pastor May Review with the Couple

1. Marriage is a wonderful gift. There is no other experience in the human endeavor quite like the experience of marriage. Husbands and wives share things on the deepest level of human exchange. In all the experience of wonder regarding marriage, couples must remember that God is the one who created marriage, the one who blesses every marriage, and the one who will bless their marriage.

2. Marriage is a very old institution. It is the oldest rite of humankind. It dates back to ancient times, and biblically speaking, it dates to the very beginning. Those who are marrying are joining an extremely long tradition.

3. There is a purpose in marriage; it exists for a reason, not simply out of convenience. It is a way of life ordered by God. Having been ordered by God, it is a divine rather than merely a human institution. Some of the purposes of marriage include:

Companionship — it is not good for anyone to be alone.
Sharing joys as well as trials.
Finding comfort in every walk of life — joy, sorrow, sickness, health.
The ordering of family life.
The birth and nurturing of children.
Finding expressions of love, tenderness, intimacy.
Realizing a sense of belonging.

4. Those who have come to the marriage celebration have come with a purpose:

> To offer the couple their prayers and support.
> To ask God's blessings.
> To witness the marriage.
> To share the joy.

5. There is a mystery in marriage. The mystery is that two people are joined together and become one. That mystery finds expression in many ways. While the two remain separate individuals, they begin to take on some of the characteristics, thoughts, even personalities of one another. The mystery takes focus in the birth of children who "magically" reflect the images of their parents in appearance, personality, intelligence, interests, innate abilities, and even gestures and body movement.

6. The mystery of marriage reflects the mystery of Christ and the church. Just as Christ and the church are one, so are husband and wife one.

7. Christ is present in marriage. Not only is Christ present, he rejoices in the happiness that husbands and wives find in one another. Christ attended the wedding celebration at Cana in Galilee where he performed his first miracle by turning the water into wine, and Christ will attend the wedding of the couple to be married. He will be the unseen, but ever-present guest not only at the wedding, but in the home the couple is to establish.

READING OF THE SCRIPTURES

Almost every wedding service calls for the reading of scripture. There is a wealth of suggested scriptures that relate to husbands and wives, love and marriage, Christ's presence in the home, our hope in Christ, the life of a Christian, and the call to rejoice. The pastor should review a number of scripture options with the couple, but insist that they select the passages they would like read at their wedding. Having them select the passages will cause them to read the passages and offer the occasion for the pastor to review the meaning of the passage with the couple. Some suggested passages include:

The creation of man and woman	Genesis 1:26-28, 31; 2:18-24
The joy of one's beloved	Song of Solomon 2:8-13
God calls you by name	Isaiah 43:1-7
God who is like a husband never forsakes	Isaiah 54:5-8
Rejoicing in the Lord	Isaiah 61:10-11
Faithfulness of God	Hosea 2:16-23
God is for us	Romans 8:31-39
Qualities of love	Romans 12:9-18
Love as the greatest virtue	I Corinthians 13
New creations in Christ	II Corinthians 5:14-20

Immeasurable riches of God's grace	Ephesians 2:4-23
Christ dwelling in you	Ephesians 3:14-21
Walking in love like Christ	Ephesians 5:2, 21-33
Reflecting the image of Christ	Philippians 2:1-8
Rejoicing in Christ	Philippians 4:4-8
Marks of a Christian	Colossians 3:12-17
Mutual respect of husbands and wives	I Peter 3:1-9
Love expressed in deeds	I John 3:18-24
Mirroring God's love	I John 4:7-16
Building a house on the solid rock	Matthew 7:24-27
Two shall become as one	Matthew 19:3-6
The greatest commandment	Matthew 22:35-40
What God has joined together	Mark 10:6-9
The marriage feast	John 2:1-11
Love one another	John 15:9-17

Focus Points the Pastor May Review with the Couple
1. What was the main point of the scripture passage selected?

2. What was it about this passage that caused the couple to select it?

3. How might this passage be applicable to their marriage?

DECLARATION OF INTENTION

B: Pastor: N_____, will you take N_____ to be your wedded wife,
promising to love her, to comfort her in time of sorrow,
to care for her in times of sickness, and to be her true and faithful husband
as long as you both shall live?

Groom: **I will.**

N _____, will you take N_____ to be your wedded husband,
promising to love him, to comfort him in times of sorrow,
to care for him in times of sickness, and
to be his faithful and true wife as long as you both shall live?

Bride: **I will.**

P: Pastor: N_____, understanding that God has created, ordered, and
blessed the covenant of marriage, do you affirm your desire and intention
to enter this covenant?

Groom : **I do.**

Pastor: N _____, understanding that God has created, ordered, and blessed the covenant of marriage, do you affirm your desire and intention to enter this covenant?

Bride: **I do.**

UM: Pastor: I ask you now, in the presence of God and these people,
to declare your intention
to enter into union with each other through the grace of Jesus Christ,
who calls you into union with himself
as acknowledged by your baptism.

Pastor to woman:

N_____, will you have N_____ to be your husband,
    to live together in holy marriage?
Will you love him, comfort him, honor and keep him,
    in sickness and in health,
and forsaking all others, be faithful to him
    as long as you both shall live?

Woman: **I will.**

Pastor to man:

N_____, will you have N_____ to be your wife,
    to live together in holy marriage?
Will you love her, comfort her, honor and keep her,
    in sickness and in health,
and forsaking all others, be faithful to her
    as long as you both shall live?

Man: **I will.**

UCC: Pastor: Before God and this congregation,
I ask you to affirm your willingness
to enter this covenant of marriage
and to share all the joys and sorrows
of this relationship,
whatever the future may hold.

Pastor to Groom:

N _____, will you have N_____ to be your wife,
and will you love her faithfully
as long as you both shall live?

Groom: **I will, with the help of God.**

Pastor to Bride:

N _____, will you have N_____ to be your husband,
and will you love him faithfully
as long as you both shall live?

Bride: **I will, with the help of God.**

Focus Points the Pastor May Review with the Couple

1. There is an enormous difference between a marriage solemnized in a civil ceremony and one solemnized in the church. A civil ceremony is a ceremony whose vows are merely before men, be that a judge or magistrate. A Christian ceremony held before a pastor and in the church is a marriage whose covenant is made before God. What an enormous difference between the two ceremonies and the veracity on which the vows stand.

2. Marriage in the Christian context is a holy union. It is a union that recognizes God as the creator and giver of life and Christ as the Redeemer. It is a union whose foundation is the Lord and recognizes his presence in all of life, but especially in the marriage and home.

3. Marriage is God's idea. God created, ordered, and blessed the covenant of marriage. Marriage, while a human institution, transcends any human understanding or legal requirement as those married in Christ are bound by the one who designed the holy covenant.

4. There will be "bumps in the road," and acknowledging those bumps up front will enable couples to understand life and marriage are no bed of roses. Yet the marital covenant is to share "the joys and the sorrows" in whatever circumstance the future may hold. The couple is to comfort one another, honor and keep one another in sickness and in health, and in every other unexpected circumstance. Here is the pastor's opportunity to allow the couple to see marriage not only as a permanent bond, but one that sees them through both the trials and good fortunes of life.

5. This is a permanent relationship. The vow states that it is one that lasts "as long as we both shall live." Here the pastor may wish to discuss the meaning of permanence in marriage, that the vows are not taken just for a season, but taken for the future until one of the two passes away. The vows have no sense of confinement; quite the contrary, as the vows are sources of strength that the one to whom we are married will be there through all of life's experiences until the very end, just as we will be there for them. While we never know what the future may hold, knowing our wife or husband will be there with us through it all is a source of great reassurance. Such assurance is part of the covenant.

AFFIRMATION OR PLEDGE OF SUPPORT OF FAMILIES

B: Pastor: Who gives this woman to be married to this man?

Escort of the Bride: **I do**

Or   Escort of the Bride: **Her mother and I do.**

P: Pastor (Addressing the family members): N _____, N_____, do you give your blessing to N_____ and N _____, and promise to do everything in your power to uphold them in their marriage?

Families: **We (I) give our (my) blessing and promise our (my) loving support.**

Or   Families: **We do.**

UM: Pastor to the people: The marriage of N_____ and N_____ unites their families and creates a new one.
They ask for your blessing.

Parents or a representative of the parents: **We rejoice in your union, and pray God's blessings upon you.**

Pastor: Do you who represent their families rejoice in their union and pray God's blessing upon them?

Families: **We do.**

For blended families, children of the couple may say:

We love both of you.
We bless your marriage.
Together we will be a family.

Pastor to the people: Will all of you, by God's grace, do everything in your power to uphold and care for these two persons in their marriage?

People: **We will.**

UCC: For blended families: Pastor to children: N_____, N_____, and N_____, you are entering a new family.
Will you give this new
family your trust, love, and affection?

Each Child: **I will.**

Pastor addressing the bride and groom: N_____ and N_____, will you be faithful and loving parents to N_____, N_____, and N_____?

Couple: **We will.**

Pastor addressing the families: Will the families of N_____ and N_____ please stand in support of this couple? Do you offer your prayerful blessing and loving support of this marriage? If so, please say, "I do."

Family Members: **I do.**

Pastor addressing the guests: Do you as the people of God, pledge your support and encouragement to the covenant commitment that N_____ and N_____ are making together? If so, please say, "We do."

People: **We do.**

Focus Points the Pastor May Review with the Couple

1. It is important to have the support of both families as the new couple is an extension of their previous family. This part of the service gives families an opportunity to participate in the service and visually and verbally show their support for the marriage.

2. Allowing the guests to show their support for the marriage gives the guests an opportunity to participate in the service as well as offer their affirmation.

3. Allowing children who are children of previous marriages to participate gives the children an opportunity not only to participate, but to show their support. In cases where children are having difficulty with the new marriage, such participation may allow them the opportunity to move forward with their emotions. However, no child should be coerced into making a statement of approval if he/she is uncomfortable in so doing. The pastor should discuss this point with the parents when reviewing the service in order that a child not be embarrassed or put on the spot.

VOWS OF THE MARRIAGE COVENANT

B: The pastor asks the couple to join right hands and to face each other.

Pastor requests that the groom repeat after him.

I, N _____, take thee, N_____, to be my wedded wife,
to have and to hold
from this day forward,
for better, for worse,
for richer, for poorer,
in sickness and in health,
to love and to cherish,
until death us do part.

Pastor requests that the bride repeat after him.

I, N _____, take thee, N _____, to be my wedded husband,
to have and to hold
from this day forward,
for better, for worse,
for richer, for poorer,
in sickness and in health,
to love and to cherish,
until death us do part.

P: The pastor addresses the couple with these words:

N_____ and N_____, since it is your intention to marry,
join your right hands,
and with your promises bind yourselves to each
other as husband and wife.

The groom repeats these vows after the pastor:

I, N_____, take you, N _____, to be my wife;
and I promise,
before God and these witnesses,
to be your loving and faithful husband;
in plenty and in want;
in joy and in sorrow;
in sickness and in health;
as long as we both shall live.

The bride then repeats these vows after the pastor:

I, N_____, take you, N_____, to be my husband,
and I promise
before God and these witnesses,
to be your loving and faithful wife;
in plenty and in want,
in joy and in sorrow;
in sickness and in health;
as long as we both shall live.

UM: The couple, facing each other and joining hands, repeat after the pastor.

Groom: In the name of God,
I, N_____, take you, N_____, to be my wife,
to have and to hold
from this day forward,
for better, for worse,
for richer, for poorer,
in sickness and in health,
to love and to cherish,
until we are parted by death.
This is my solemn vow.

Bride: In the name of God,
I, N_____, take you, N_____, to be my husband,
to have and to hold
from this day forward,
for better, for worse,
for richer, for poorer,
in sickness and in health,
to love and to cherish,
until we are parted by death.
This is my solemn vow.

UCC: The pastor invites the bride and groom to join hands and face each other, repeating the vows after the pastor.

Bride: N_____, I give myself to you
to be your wife.
I promise to love and sustain you
in the covenant of marriage,
from this day forward,

in sickness and in health,
in plenty and in want,
in joy and in sorrow,
as long as we both shall live.

Groom: N_____, I give myself to you
to be your husband.
I promise to love and sustain you
in the covenant of marriage,
from this day forward,
in sickness and in health,
in plenty and in want,
in joy and in sorrow,
as long as we both shall live.

Focus Points the Pastor May Review with the Couple

1. The vows are made before God and the witnesses who are gathered. A vow is different from a mere promise. A vow is a solemn assertion that binds oneself. A vow is something that should not be broken. A vow has a sacred promise.

2. The marital covenant begins the moment the vow is spoken and continues into the future until one of the couple passes away. The words, "from this day forward," are found in most marriage ceremonies and define the beginning of the life-long relationship.

3. The gift of one's self is the ultimate gift. The gift of the self exceeds all earthly treasure. The gift of one's own being, all that one is or hopes to be, is truly the most precious gift one can give.

4. Life is uncertain. No one knows what tomorrow holds. It may be a tomorrow of bounty and plenty or it may be a tomorrow of need. Life may always be filled with good health, unending happiness, without trial or tragedy, or it may have the unexpected crosses of illness, accident, sorrow, hardship, pain, want , and need. Life may have peak to peak experiences, or it may have the shadows of the valleys of hardship. It may be better or it may be worse. It may be richer or it may be poorer. It may be a glass that is always full or it may be a glass that is often empty or somewhere between full and empty.

No one knows what the future holds. There are no guarantees. Even the best laid plans and most impeccable preparation do not ensure a life that is trouble free.

When couples envision their future with their lives before them, all of life seems blissful and good, filled with rainbows, sunshine, and dreams. There is a feeling of standing on tiptoe gazing into a future without limit, trial, or burden. Yet the reality is that sooner or later, adversity comes to everyone. The vows of marriage are "prototype" for whatever circumstance, good or bad, blessing or misfortune, star or scar, life may bring a couple. While "for better, for worse, for richer, for poorer, in sickness and in health," does not cover every possible condition a couple might encounter, these words are meant to represent the entire spectrum of possibilities of fate and fortune. The vow taken by the marrying couple is that whatever circumstance they may find themselves facing, each will uphold the covenantal vow to love, sustain, have, and hold, until they are parted by death.

Vows are the bedrock of marriage. They are the ultimate affirmation that the one to whom the vows are spoken will not be forsaken in times of trial or uncertainty and will be the one with whom joy and love are shared in times when life smiles upon them with showers of blessings. The flip side is that the one to whom the vows are being spoken is reciprocating with the same covenantal promises. Such is the covenant of marriage and when kept as spoken will be the reassuring structure for strength, comfort, trust, and safe passage in the journey of life.

EXCHANGE OF RINGS OR SYMBOLS

B: The pastor invites the groom to place the wedding ring on the third finger
of the bride's left hand, and to repeat after the pastor.

Groom: N_____, with this ring, I thee wed,
in the name of the Father, and
of the Son, and of the Holy Spirit. Amen.

The pastor invites the bride to place the wedding ring on the third finger
of the groom's left hand, and to repeat after the pastor.

Bride: N_____, with this ring, I thee wed,
in the name of the Father, and
of the Son, and of the Holy Spirit. Amen.

P: Pastor asks the couple: What do you bring as a sign of your promise?

The couple presents the rings and the pastor offers the following prayer:

By your blessing, O God,
may these rings be to N_____ and N_____
symbols of unending love and faithfulness,
reminding them of the covenant they have made this day,
through Jesus Christ our Lord. Amen.

The pastor then gives the ring to the groom, requesting that he place the ring
on the bride's finger and repeat the ring vows.

Groom: N_____, I give you this ring as a sign of our covenant,
in the name of the Father,
and of the Son,
and of the Holy Spirit.

Bride: I receive this ring as a sign of our covenant,
in the name of the Father,
and of the Son,
and of the Holy Spirit.

The pastor then gives the ring to the bride to be placed on the groom's
finger, repeating the ring vows after the pastor to the groom.

Bride: N_____, I give you this ring as a sign of our covenant,
in the name of the Father,
and of the Son,
and of the Holy Spirit.

Groom: I receive this ring as a sign of our covenant,
in the name of the Father,
and of the Son,
and of the Holy Spirit.

UM: The pastor, upon taking the rings, says,

These rings are the outward and visible sign
of an inward and spiritual grace,
signifying to all the uniting of N_____ and N_____ in holy marriage.

The pastor then offers the following prayer:

Bless, O Lord, the giving of these rings,
that they who wear them may live in your peace
and continue in your favor
all the days of their life;
through Jesus Christ our Lord. Amen.

The pastor gives the ring to the groom and invites him to place it on the
bride's third finger of the left hand, repeating after the pastor.

Groom: N _____, I give you this ring,
as a sign of my vow,
and with all that I am,
and all that I have,
I honor you;
in the name of the Father,
and of the Son,
and of the Holy Spirit.

The pastor then gives the ring to the bride and invites her to place it on the groom's third finger of the left hand, repeating after the pastor.

Bride: N_____, I give you this ring,
as a sign of my vow,
and with all that I am,
and all that I have,
I honor you;
in the name of the Father,
and of the Son,
and of the Holy Spirit.

UCC: As the exchange of rings begins, the pastor asks the couple the following question:

Pastor: N_____ and N_____, what will you share to symbolize your love?

The bride and groom may name the symbols (rings) or simply place them in the hands of the pastor. The pastor holds them up and offers the following prayer:

Pastor: By these symbols of covenant promise, Gracious God, remind N_____ and N_____ of your encircling love and unending faithfulness
that in all their
life together they may know joy and peace in one another. Amen.

The pastor then hands the ring to the groom, requesting that the groom repeat the vows for the ring exchange.

Groom: N_____, I give you this ring as a sign of my love and faithfulness.

Bride: I receive this ring as a sign of our love and faithfulness.

The pastor then hands the ring to the bride, requesting that she repeat the vows of the ring exchange.

Bride: N_____, I give you this ring as a sign of my love and faithfulness.

Groom: I receive this ring as a sign of our love and faithfulness.

Focus Points the Pastor May Discuss with the Bride and Groom

1. The ring is a visible sign for all that it represents: love, faithfulness, honor, trust, union, all that a person is or hopes to be. The ring sends a message to all the world that the person wearing it is married and committed to the vows of marriage.

2. The ring has its own symbolism. It is without end, symbolizing the love the couple has for one another is also without end. It is made of gold, a very precious metal, symbolizing the supreme value of the relationship. It is pure, symbolizing the purity of the relationship, that it is to exist without spot or wrinkle, or invasion of impurity. It is a relationship built upon honor, integrity, and authenticity.

3. The ring should be worn at all times as the visible reminder to the wearer and to all others that a deep, abiding, and lasting commitment has been made and will always be honored.

DECLARATION OR ANNOUNCEMENT OF MARRIAGE

B: Pastor: For as much as this man and this woman have
promised to be faithful and true
to each other, and have witnessed the same
before God and this company by
spoken vows and by exchanging rings,
they enter now into a new estate.
As a Minister of the Gospel of Jesus Christ,
I now pronounce you are husband and
wife in the name of the Father,
and of the Son, and of the Holy Spirit.

P: Pastor: Before God and in the presence of this congregation.
N_____ and N_____ have made their solemn
vows known to each other.
They have confirmed their promises by the joining of hands
and by the giving and receiving of rings.
Therefore, I proclaim that they are now husband and wife.

Blessed be the Father and the Son and the Holy Spirit now and forever.

(The pastor joins the couple's right hands.)

Pastor: Those whom God has joined together let no one separate.

Pastor: As God's own,
clothe yourselves with compassion,
kindness, and patience,

131

forgiving each other
as the Lord has forgiven you,
and crown all these things with love,
which binds everything together in perfect harmony.

UM: The pastor requests that the couple join hands and then pronounces the following:

You have declared your consent and vows
before God and this congregation.
May God confirm your covenant
and fill you both with grace.

(The couple is asked to turn and face the congregation.)

Pastor: Now that N_____ and N_____ have given
themselves to each other by solemn vows,
with the joining of hands,
and the giving and receiving of rings,
I announce to you that they are husband and wife;
in the name of the Father,
and of the Son,
and of the Holy Spirit.
Those whom God has joined together,
Let no one put asunder. Amen.

UCC: The pastor requests that the couple join hands, addressing the congregation with these words.

Pastor: Those whom God has joined together, let no one separate.

Pastor addressing the couple: N_____ and N_____, you are
wife and husband with the blessing of Christ's church.
Be merciful in all your ways,
kind in heart,
and humble in mind.
Accept life and be most patient
and tolerant with one another.
Forgive as freely as God has forgiven you,
and, above everything else,
be truly loving.
Let the peace of Christ
rule in your hearts,

remembering that
as members of one body
you are called to live in harmony,
and never forget to be
thankful for all that God has done for you.

Focus Points the Pastor May Review with the Couple

1. The three ways the vows are confirmed:

   - the spoken vows
   - the joining of hands
   - the exchanging of rings

2. The congregation or guests serve as witnesses to the vows as they are made.

3. The pronouncement of marriage is conditioned upon the vows as they are offered, and the witness of God and the gathered witnesses.

4. The announcement is made in the name of the Trinity: the Father, the Son, and the Holy Spirit.

5. The marriage is a new estate, a new way of living, and new dimension of life, blessed and empowered by the Spirit of God.

6. "Those whom God has joined together, let no one separate," are the words of Jesus and may be found in Matthew 19:6. It is God who joins couples together. It is God who creates the mystery of two becoming as one. Since the act of marriage is sacred and holy, instituted and blessed by God, no one should do anything to bring it harm, discredit, disharmony, disunion, or destruction.

7. The marriage has the blessing of Christ's church. There is a marked distinction between a civil and a Christian wedding. The civil wedding makes no claim the marriage will be blessed by Christ or the church. The Christian wedding is empowered by the Spirit of Christ and his church, and having made their vows before an ordained pastor and before the people of God who serve as witnesses, the claim can be made that the marriage does indeed have the blessing of the church.

   The blessing of the church is a blessing that should neither be given nor received without thought, prayer, and serious consideration. It is not a flippant, frivolous bequest. It is given after the pastor, through the process of counsel and due preparation of the couple, after examining their readiness for marriage, and after having found no cause why they should not be duly married in the church, feels the blessing is so warranted.

8. The marriage should in every way reflect the virtues of the Christian life in terms of mercy, humility, patience, tolerance, forgiveness, and love. The couple should treat one another with the same love and honor by which Christ has treated them.

9. The husband and wife are now members of one body and as such must live in peace and in harmony.

PRAYERS OF BLESSING AND THANKSGIVING

Each marriage service incorporates a prayer of blessing or thanksgiving. Pastors should review the prayers that will be used so that the couple will have a sense of what is spoken in time of prayer.

SACRAMENT OF HOLY COMMUNION

The various services may incorporate the Sacrament of Holy Communion. Various words and liturgies of the separate traditions and communions will be used to celebrate the sacrament. The pastor need not review the focus points of the sacrament since it is an ongoing service of the church and not a part of the wedding vows as such. The pastor may counsel the couple that the celebration of the sacrament is their first act of marriage and as such symbolic of the place of Christ and their faith in the home they are to establish.

BENEDICTION AND BLESSING

The wedding service should conclude with a blessing or benediction. The pastor may offer a personal blessing or use one from the liturgy of his/her church.

B: N_____ and N_____, may Almighty God send you
his light and truth all the days of your life. May the hand of
God protect you, and his holy angels accompany you.
In the name of Jesus Christ our Lord. Amen.

P: The grace of God attend you,
the love of God surround you,
the Holy Spirit keep you,
that you may live in faith,
abound in hope,
and grow in love,
both now and forevermore. Amen.

UM: Pastor to husband and wife: God the Eternal keep you in love
with each other, so that the peace of Christ may abide in your
home. Go to serve God and your neighbor in all that you do.

Pastor to the congregation: Bear witness to the love of God in
this world, so that those to whom love is a stranger
will find you generous friends.

The grace of the Lord Jesus Christ,
the love of God,
and the communion of the Holy Spirit
be with you all. Amen.

UCC: Pastor to couple: Go forth in the love of God;
go forth in hope and in joy,
knowing that God is with you always.
And the peace of God,
which passes all understanding,
keep your hearts and minds
in the knowledge
and love of God
and of Jesus Christ;
and the blessing of God,
Creator, Redeemer, and Sanctifier, be with you,
and remain with you always. Amen.

Focus Points the Pastor May Share with the Couple

1. The blessing is a gift from the church. A blessing or benediction is a pronouncement of God's presence, love, and grace, given to the couple on behalf of the church as empowered by the ordination of the pastor. In Old and New Testament times, words set things into motion. The blessing from the pastor and church are gifts to set in motion a life of peace, harmony, hope, and joy.

2. God is truly the light on the pathways of the bride and groom as they journey through life together. God alone is the one who is able to hold and keep the couple in his love and care.

Concluding the Session

The pastor may close the session by reviewing the main points covered and answering any questions regarding the ceremony. Opportunity should be given for the bride and groom to ask any question or clarify any concern as the time for the wedding is drawing near.

Special support sessions have been prepared for "special needs marriages," that is second marriages after divorce, interfaith or mixed marriages, and second marriages after the death of a first spouse. These special needs sessions are designed to enable couples to understand their special needs situation, whether a second marriage or a mixed marriage.

If either or both partners in the marriage has/have been married before and divorced, the handout, "Profiling the Marriage That Intentionally Ended," should be given with the request that it be filled out and brought to the special session. If both were divorced, both should receive the handout. The handout, "Able to Love Again," should be given persons whose first marriage ended with the death of a spouse. The "Blended Family Assessment" should be filled out by both the prospective bride and groom, and along with either "Profiling the Marriage That Intentionally Ended," or "Able to Love Again," brought back to optional special needs session.

If the proposed marriage is a "Mixed Marriage," that is an interfaith or racially mixed marriage, the handouts on Mixed Marriages should be given with the request that they be returned for review in special session on Mixed Marriages.

The session may close with prayer reflective of the wedding service and the meaning of the vows discussed.

Sample Closing Prayers

You are the God of all that is good, O Lord. Today we are especially conscious of your goodness as we draw nearer to the wonderful event of the marriage of N_____ and N_____. We remember not only that you planned and ordained marriage, but that you are present in the wedding ceremony itself, just as you were present in the wedding celebration in Cana of Galilee. With the wedding so near at hand, our hearts are jumping with joy, knowing that our journey of courtship is coming to an end and our journey of marriage is about to begin. May you be especially present in this wedding celebration that all who are gathered may feel your blessing in the life of this man and woman. In your name we make this and every prayer. Amen.

Eternal God, as we approach the wedding day of N_____ and N_____, we recall our time together in every aspect of planning this great and glorious celebration. It is with hearts full of joy and gladness that we stand on tiptoe looking to that day that is approaching so rapidly. As pastor, I thank you for these two special people. What a blessing in my life it has been to come to know them and share with them in these days of planning and preparation. Today, we thank you for the upcoming wedding service itself, knowing that it will not only be a service of beauty, but one of worship and meaning. Be especially near to these two in the coming days. Calm their fears and elevate their joys. This we ask in your name. Amen.

Part III

**Special Support
for the Pastor
and Optional Sessions**

Special Support and Optional Sessions

Points for the Pastor

These additional or optional sessions are designed as support for the pastor in special needs settings: interfaith marriages, interracial marriages, marriages after divorce, and marriages after the death of a spouse. They are called special because each entails some issues that would not be found in first time marriages or marriages in which there is no interfaith or interracial issue. It is recommended that these special needs concerns be addressed as there is no better place to address them than in the confidence of the premarital interview with the pastor.

Concerns to Be Considered by the Pastor

- **Interfaith marriages**

- **Racially mixed marriages**

- **Second marriages after divorce**

- **Second marriages after the death of a spouse**

Optional Session I

Mixed or Interfaith Marriages

(Helping Couples Integrate Faith and Cultural Traditions)

Life in the twenty-first century is in dramatic transition, but no where is transition more pronounced than in the once homogenous communities across the land, communities where everyone knew everyone, where those born there, grew up there, married the person down the street, settled down to raise a family, and died there, only to see the cycle repeat itself. Such was true not only in small towns, but even in larger cities where people seemed to congregate in static communities that centered around the institutions which intrinsically kept them local.

Such homogeneity kept life inbred. People knew people and relationships were built upon long-standing histories of acquaintances and associations. Few thought about venturing beyond the comfort zone of a life of familiarity. Things felt good as they were, so why bother changing. Even the kids that left home and went away to college or military service returned to their roots, and married the girl or boy down the street, because doing so just seemed the right thing to do. That girl or boy went to the same church or at least the church across the street, the same school or at least a rival school across town, and everyone gathered at the same drugstore or hangout. While it may not have been John Boy and the Waltons, or Barney and Mayberry RFD, or even Fonzie, it was a scene and a way of life where everything seemed to be in place.

Things have changed! Life is not as it used to be. Life is much bigger and far more complex than anyone might have ever imagined. The towns became cities. The cities became metropolises. Old-line familiarity gave way to the idiosyncratic unfamiliar. Life began to feel different and the experience of the new felt strange and distant. The once pastoral scene of life became a multifaceted collage of people, institutions, and traditions, all not only clamoring for space, but also making their marks on the playing field. It would be an understatement and much too simplistic to say that we live in a pluralistic society. The mixing of peoples in the face-to-face encounters of society stretches even the imagination of what may be meant by the term *pluralism*.

Face-to-face, that's the term, and such are the dynamics descriptive of life today. Unlike the world of only a couple of decades ago, it is a world of mixing and blending, blending and mixing. The interfacing begins around the tables and on the playgrounds of nursery schools, but catapults into grade and high school, college, and the work place. Such integrations of cultures and traditions allows people to see others not so much as different, but more as the same. Jericho's walls of "us" and "them" have come tumbling down.

Add to this mix the effect of the media, especially television. The once clearly defined primary group, the once clear line of demarcation of "we" and "they," is no longer so clearly marked. Definitions of the reference group have changed. Even cultural subgroups who have historically set parameters of definition of "us" and "them," are finding it much more difficult to hold boundaries in place.

The demographics of America have changed and all that right before our eyes. The settlement of America by the immigration mostly of northern and eastern Europeans and those brought to the shores in shackles to be sold as slaves has given way to an influx of Hispanics, who like their predecessors are looking for opportunity and a better life. So much has this most recent wave of immigration affected the demographics of the land that now Hispanics outnumber Euro-Americans in the State of California. Add to this the influx of Asian and Middle Eastern immigrants, and one begins to see America as the true melting pot of the world.

Into such settings, boy still meets girl, but she may not be the girl next door or down the street or even across town. She may not even be "one of us" as defined by religion, racial or ethnic group, political preference, or social status. She may not have come from our country or even our continent, and her family traditions and cultural values may seem quite strange, or at least they are quite different from the seemingly unchanging mores of yesteryear.

Boy not only meets girl, but boy and girl fall in love, and love has that quality of transcending many other virtues and values. Perhaps the Apostle Paul said it best when he said, *"Love bears all things, believes all things, hopes all things, endures all things"* (I Corinthians 13:7). Love does bear all things and sometimes other principles and ideologies find themselves taking a back seat to this the greatest of virtues.

Given the paradigm we have just described, people for whom love has transcended custom, tradition, and value will want to formalize and legalize that relationship in bonds of marriage. They will want their relationship celebrated and blessed in their traditions of faith and places of worship. They will also call upon their religious guide/leader to understand and appreciate their love as well as to hear their vows.

Pastors will therefore be called upon more and more to marry persons out of differing faith, racial, and ethnic backgrounds. Pastors need to be knowledgeable of church doctrine of faith and practice of mixed marriages as well equip themselves to minister to such couples who wish to be married. More importantly, enabling prospective mixed marriage couples to understand and process the parameters of mixed marriage is a task needful and incumbent for the pastor. This session will review three of the most common occurrences of mixed marriages: Protestant — Catholic, Protestant — Jewish, and those racially mixed, namely, Black — White. Focus on these forms is not to the exclusion of other forms. These are simply the most prevalent.

Protestant — Catholic Marriages

The most common form of mixed marriages is the marriage of Protestants and Catholics. The two church communions view mixed marriages quite differently, but differences are far more defined in the *Code of Canon Law* of the Catholic Church than may be found in any books of discipline or orders of faith and practice in the various communions of Protestantism. Germane to the whole issue is the fact that within Catholicism, marriage is a sacrament; whereas in Protestantism, marriage is a rite or covenant, but not a sacrament. Herein, lies the disparity. Just as a point of review, within Catholicism there are seven sacraments: Baptism, Confirmation, Eucharist, Penance, Anointing the Sick, Orders (ordination), and Marriage. Within Protestantism there are two sacraments: Baptism and the Eucharist or Holy Communion.

Since marriage is a sacrament in the Catholic Church, as one might expect, it is treated quite differently than in Protestantism. The *Code of Canon Law* defines marriage, the obligations of those married, and all the parameters of marriage according to canon law. It should be noted that there is more code for the sacrament of marriage than any other sacrament, which is reflective of the importance of this sacrament in the life of the Church. Canons 1055-1165 are rules defining and governing the sacrament.

Most canon law defining and regulating the governance of marriage today is based on the 1917 Code. However, from time to time the Church may study and revise its canon law as it did in 1983 when Pope John Paul appointed a commission of cardinals and bishops to study the canon again and make recommendations for revision as needed. Only the Holy Father has the authority to confirm the recommended changes.

Here follows several of the canons and commentary as they pertain to marriage.

The definition of marriage is found in Canon 1055. **The matrimonial covenant, by which a man and a woman establish between themselves a partnership of the whole of life, is by its nature ordered toward the good of the spouses and the procreation and education of offspring; this covenant between baptized persons has been raised by Christ the Lord to the dignity of sacrament.**[7]

This canon is based on the Old Testament Jewish definition of a covenant, and as such marriage is a relationship that does not cease even if the consent to the covenant is withdrawn by one or both parties, quite a different understanding from the Protestant perspective or civil law.[8]

Canon 1056: **The essential properties of marriage are unity and indissolubility, which in Christian marriage obtain a special firmness in virtue of the sacrament.**[9]

Marriage, even in its natural form apart from church law, promotes unity. Indissolubility is an essential part of the marriage covenant.

Canon 1059 states: **Even if only one party is Catholic, the marriage of Catholics is regulated not only by divine law but also by canon law.**[10]

The Catholic Church believes that the church as the visible structure of Christ's body on earth has authority over marriage. Such authority is exercised over the baptized, but also extends to the non-baptized if they are entering a marriage where one partner is a baptized Catholic. Protestants may have difficulty embracing this law because they either fail to understand the meaning of the canon or disagree with its position.[11]

Canon 1066: **Before marriage is celebrated, it must be evident that nothing stands in the way of its valid and licit celebration.**[12]

This law requires that the priest be certain that nothing stands in the way of a valid marriage. Concerns which may stand in the way include such issues as emotional disorders, outright refusal to have children, or rejection of the Catholic concept of marriage. There is no such thing as "voluntary childlessness" in Catholicism since one purpose of marriage (Canon 1055) is the procreation of children. Hence, the Catholic position on marriage and birth control.

Canon 1069: **All the faithful are obliged to reveal any impediments they are aware of to the pastor or to the local ordinary before the celebration of marriage.**[13]

An impediment is a condition which directly affects marriage in such a way that the persons by law would not be allowed to marry. These include impediments of divine law and impediments of ecclesiastical law. Divine law impediments are inclusive of all persons who marry, baptized or not. Ecclesiastical impediments are based on the sacramental nature of marriage. Examples of impediments would include incestuous marriage, marriages to non-believers, and second marriages after divorce. For example, if a Catholic did not inform the priest his/her betrothed was a non-believer or that he/she had been married and divorced, such would be an impediment and the marriage declared null and void by the laws of the church.[14]

Canons 1124-1129 address the concern of "Mixed Marriages," that is from the Catholic perspective, marriages between Catholics and non-baptized persons and marriages between Catholics and baptized non-Catholics. The concern of the Catholic Church for marriage between Catholics and either the non-baptized or the baptized who were not Catholics, was the concern over the continued practice of the faith by the Catholic and the baptism and rearing of children born to the union, that is that the children be raised as Catholics. Canons pertinent to Catholics marrying non-Catholics and to the conditions under which such marriages may be granted by the church are Canon 1124 and Canon 1125

Canon 1124 states: **Without the express permission of the competent authority, marriage is forbidden between two baptized persons, one of whom was baptized in the Catholic Church or received into it after baptism and has not left it by formal act, and the other of whom is a member of a church or ecclesiastical community which is not in full communion with the Catholic Church.**[15]

By canonical definition, mixed marriages involving Catholics are either those marriages between baptized non-Catholics or those who have not been baptized at all.

In order for a Catholic to be granted permission to marry either, a dispensation must be granted by the bishop as recommended by the local pastor or priest. In requesting the dispensation the priest must state the reasons for the request, which may include: 1) The spiritual welfare of the faithful, 2) The hope that the non-Catholic will enter full communion with the Church (Catholic), 3) Danger of attempted invalid marriage, 4) Scarcity of Catholics, or 5) Other reasons cited[16] The dispensation states that it is not permissible to have two marriage services, one Catholic and one non-Catholic or that the two services be collapsed into one. Participation in the Catholic service by Protestant clergy requires a dispensation from the bishop and the Protestant pastor may then participate only on a limited basis. Only the priest can "hear" the vows.

The second requirement in obtaining a dispensation for a mixed marriage involves conditions on which the marriage may take place. These conditions are delineated in Canon 1125.

The local ordinary can grant this permission if there is a just and reasonable cause; he is not to grant it unless the following conditions have been fulfilled: the Catholic party declares

that he or she is prepared to remove dangers of falling away from the faith and makes a sincere promise to do all in his or her power to have all the children baptized and brought up in the Catholic Church; the other party is to be informed at an appropriate time of these promises which the Catholic party has to make, so that it is clear that the other party is truly aware of the promise and obligation of the Catholic party; both parties are to be instructed on the essential ends and properties of marriage, which are not to be excluded by either party.[17]

A just and reasonable cause is not simply the couple's desire to be married. The priest where the marriage is to take place determines the validity of the just cause as based on information presented to the priest. Generally, if the above conditions are met, permission for a mixed marriage is granted.

A prospective Catholic bride or groom who proposes to marry a non-Catholic may petition the Catholic Church for a dispensation from canonical form in order for the marriage to take place before a non-Catholic pastor. If the dispensation is granted, the Catholic priest may be present for the ceremony, but may not "hear" or give consent to the wedding vows. Reasons for such a dispensation may include: 1) Instances when a non-Catholic has a conscientious objection to a Catholic celebration; 2) When there is a possibility of estrangement from the non-Catholic party's family or religious denomination; 3) When the non-Catholic party requests a parent or close family relative to perform the wedding.

Protestant pastors may have difficulty understanding the canonical laws of the Catholic Church governing marriage since the two traditions approach marriage from different rules of faith and practice. Conversely, Catholics may wonder about the more liberal approaches of the denominations of Protestantism relative to the canonical laws of the Catholic Church. There are a few questions that are often asked by Protestants other than those covered above in the brief overview of the canons reviewed. Perhaps the Question and Answer approach will shed some light on these questions.

Question: What is an annulment?
Answer: An annulment is a statement granted by the bishop of a diocese that declares a marriage as null and void. The bishop grants the annulment for various reasons, but mainly it is granted because the sacramental bond had an impediment and therefore did not exist. The bishop, through his delegate or a tribunal, investigates the marriage for such impediments, and based on the findings and recommendations, determines the just cause for an annulment. Children born to a marriage prior to the annulment are not born out of wedlock, since the marriage had an impediment and at the time of the birth of the children had not been declared null.

Question: Can a Catholic remarry after divorce?
Answer: A Catholic cannot marry a person who is divorced. The non-Catholic party must go through the annulment process the same as the Catholic.

Question: How does divorce affect membership in the Catholic Church?
Answer: It does not so long as the person does not re-marry. A divorced person who remarries cannot receive the sacrament of holy communion.[18]

Protestants see marriage as a covenantal commitment that has its foundation in the faithfulness of God's love. The wedding service is the glad celebration in which two people unite as husband

144

and wife in the mutual exchange of covenantal promises. The presiding pastor represents the church and gives the marriage the church's blessing. Since marriage is not a sacrament in the Protestant church, the perspective of marriage is quite different than in the Catholic as is the concept of "mixed marriage" between Catholics and Protestants.

When couples from Catholic and Protestant communions approach the Protestant pastor requesting marriage, it is incumbent upon the pastor not only to be knowledgeable of Catholic laws governing mixed marriage, but also to be knowledgeable of his/her own church's discipline regarding the subject. It is also necessary for the pastor to have processed his/her own judgments and conclusions in order best to guide the couple spiritually toward the celebration of their marriage and the establishment of their home and family.

There are certain motivations that may cause the Catholic and non-Catholic parties to seek the celebration of their wedding before a Protestant pastor or within a Protestant church. These may include:

- The Catholic party may be only nominally a Catholic while the Protestant may be a devout Protestant.

- The Protestant may consciously object to a Catholic celebration.

- The families of the Protestant may object to a Catholic wedding and such would cause grave alienation.

- The Protestant may not be willing to allow his/her spouse-to-be to take the vow to raise the children in the Catholic Church.

- The couple may not be willing to accept the position of the Catholic Church regarding the procreation of children as the purpose of marriage. Some Protestant couples have agreed to be voluntarily childless for various reasons, such as career or personal interests.

- One or both parties may be divorced and not wish to go through the process of annulment.

- From the Catholic partner's perspective, there may be a hidden impediment the person does not wish to reveal.

- There may not be a Catholic pastor or church available due to the scarcity of Catholics in some communities.

- The couple may have concluded it would be in the best interest of the marriage to be in the same church and by mutual consent the decision was reached that the church of preference was a Protestant communion.

- The couple may be worshiping in a Protestant church.

- The officiating Protestant pastor may be a relative or friend of one of the persons to be married. Going through the process of getting a dispensation to allow the Protestant pastor to participate in the Catholic service may be too cumbersome or difficult.

- The pastoral care and other requirements that must precede a celebration of marriage in the Catholic Church (Canons 1063ff) are perceived as too arduous or required records may not be available. The requirements include:

  A certificate of baptism from the baptismal church.

  Records of communion.

  Six months' notice of the upcoming celebration to be given to the diocese by the marrying priest.

  Premarital instruction by the priest, deacon, or team.

  Record of confirmation.

  Completed paperwork.

Groom's Interfaith Marriage Assessment

(Practical Concerns in Protestant — Catholic Marriages)

The following survey is intended to reflect your feelings on issues surrounding your upcoming interfaith marriage representing the Protestant and Catholic traditions. Please take a moment to fill out the requested responses, being as honest as you can regarding the concerns addressed. Remember, your responses will enable the pastor to bring focus in your next session to the concerns you have listed.

1. Have you and your fiancée discussed any of the concerns that might be involved in your upcoming Protestant — Catholic marriage? What are some issues you have thought about?

_____

_____

2. Have you discussed the implications of an interfaith marriage?

    a. _____ A great deal?

    b. _____ Somewhat?

    c. _____ Hardly at all?

3. Are there concerns about your fiancée's faith tradition that concern you? _____

_____

4. Do you feel there are things about your faith tradition that concern your fiancée? _____

_____

5. Have you attended worship at your fiancée's church? _____

6. If you have attended worship at your fiancée's church, how did it feel? _____

_____

7. Are there things about your fiancée's religious heritage you do not understand? _____

_____

8. Do you feel there are a lot of similarities between the Protestant and the Catholic Church?

_____

_____

9. Are there any striking differences? _____

_____

10. If your fiancée would not want to join your church, how would you feel about joining hers?

_____

11. What effect, if any, will your separate church traditions have on your marriage? _____

_____

12. Would you say you are:

_____ Highly committed to your church's heritage, practices, and beliefs?

_____ Nominally committed?

_____ Church heritage, practice, and doctrines are not so important.

13. Would it be a concern to your family that you are entering an interfaith marriage?

_____ My family is very concerned.

_____ My family accepts the marriage with reservation.

_____ It doesn't matter at all.

14. How do you feel about having your children raised in your wife-to-be's church? _____

_____

T for True — F for False

_____ We have rather thoroughly talked through the issues of our upcoming interfaith marriage.

_____ Our families are comfortable with our upcoming mixed marriage.

_____ The vow to have our children raised Catholic bothers me.

_____ We understand the differences between the Catholic and the Protestant church regarding "the procreation of children" as a reason for marriage.

_____ There is nothing that would prevent us from being married in the Catholic Church.

_____ We are comfortable remaining in our separate churches after marriage.

_____ We have discussed being members of the same church.

_____ We enjoy worshiping in each other's churches.

Bride's Interfaith Marriage Assessment

(Practical Concerns in Protestant — Catholic Marriages)

The following survey is intended to reflect your feelings on issues surrounding your upcoming interfaith marriage representing the Protestant and Catholic traditions. Please take a moment to fill out the requested responses, being as honest as you can regarding the concerns addressed. Remember, your responses will enable the pastor to bring focus in your next session to the concerns you have listed.

1. Have you and your fiancé discussed any of the concerns that might be involved in your upcoming Protestant — Catholic marriage? What are some issues you have thought about?

_____

_____

2. Have you discussed the implications of an interfaith marriage?

    a. _____ A great deal?

    b. _____ Somewhat?

    c. _____ Hardly at all?

3. Are there concerns about your fiancé's faith tradition that concern you? _____

_____

4. Do you feel there are things about your faith tradition that concern your fiancé? _____

_____

5. Have you attended worship at your fiancé's church? _____

6. If you have attended worship at your fiancé's church, how did it feel? _____

_____

7. Are there things about your fiancé's religious heritage you do not understand? _____

_____

8. Do you feel there are a lot of similarities between the Protestant and the Catholic Church?

_____

_____

9. Are there any striking differences? _____

_____

10. If your fiancé would not want to join your church, how would you feel about joining his?

_____

11. What effect, if any, will your separate church traditions have on your marriage? _____

_____

12. Would you say you are:

_____ Highly committed to your church's heritage, practices, and beliefs?

_____ Nominally committed?

_____ Church heritage, practice, and doctrines are not so important.

13. Would it be a concern to your family that you are entering an interfaith marriage?

_____ My family is very concerned.

_____ My family accepts the marriage with reservation.

_____ It doesn't matter at all.

14. How do you feel about having your children raised in your husband-to-be's church? _____

_____

T for True — F for False

_____ We have rather thoroughly talked through the issues of our upcoming interfaith marriage.

_____ Our families are comfortable with our upcoming mixed marriage.

_____ The vow to have our children raised Catholic bothers me.

_____ We understand the differences between the Catholic and the Protestant church regarding "the procreation of children" as a reason for marriage.

_____ There is nothing that would prevent us from being married in the Catholic Church.

_____ We are comfortable remaining in our separate churches after marriage.

_____ We have discussed being members of the same church.

_____ We enjoy worshiping in each other's churches.

Christian — Jewish Marriages

Crossing the faith line between the Jewish and the Christian faiths in terms of marriage is somewhat more pronounced than an interfaith marriage between a Protestant and a Catholic. This greater differentiation comes not only from differing religious beliefs, but also from differing ethnic heritages. Such a marriage involves bringing together two separate and distinct sets of beliefs and traditions. Thus, such a marriage and wedding can be challenging. It has been suggested that so far as the wedding service is concerned, it is best to work out a service that brings together wording from both services that will not create feelings of alienation.

In the event two officiants are requested, one Christian and one Jewish, it may be a bit difficult to find a rabbi who will consent to participate. Some rabbis have strict conditions. Some refuse to officiate in a church and some require a commitment to establish a Jewish home and raise the children of the marriage as Jewish.

Bringing couples together not only from separate religious beliefs, but also from totally separate traditions can be a daunting task. Such interfaith couples should spend a great deal of time processing their different religions and traditions. It is important that the two families of the marrying couple be supportive of the marriage and every effort to involve them not only in support, but in the process itself ensures greater success the marriage will succeed.

Because there is such a wide margin of belief and tradition, pastors who participate in interfaith weddings between Jews and Christians should spend considerable time reviewing the challenges the couple may face. Important to that review would be such concerns as customs, practices, and terms that are unfamiliar from the other's tradition.

Jewish weddings can occur any day of the week except the Sabbath, days of the Jewish festivals, and the three weeks between the seventeenth day of Tammuz and the ninth of Av, and the sefirah period of the Passover.

There are several Jewish pre-wedding customs that are designed to support the bride and groom before the day of their wedding. Five of the most important customs are: Separation, Henna parties, Aufruf, Mikvah, and fasting.

Traditionally, Jewish couples **separate** for a period of time before the wedding and do not see one another until they gather under the huppah. The period of separation may last from a couple of days to a week. **Henna** parties are held for most Middle Eastern brides. The theme of these parties is for mothers of the bride to feed their daughters sweets — nothing sour, as a way of bonding between the mothers and daughters. The **Aufruf** is a Yiddish custom of calling up of the couple on the Sabbath before the wedding in which the groom recites the blessings before and after the reading of the Torah. The **Mikvah** is a ritual of immersing the bride in a mikvah or ritual bath water, followed by a party of friends and celebration. In most Jewish communities, both the bride and groom **fast** beginning at sundown the night before the wedding. The first glass of wine under the huppah signals the ending of the fast.

The Jewish wedding begins with the groom's **tish,** or table. The tish is not supposed to be serious as the groom attempts to present a talk on a portion of the reading from the Torah and his family and friends interrupt and "heckle" him. Such a setting sets a happy and jovial tone for the wedding. The **Ketubah,** marriage contract, is signed after the tish by the groom, the rabbi, and two male witnesses. Despite saying the groom has acquired his bride, the ketubah is really about the rights of the bride and the groom's responsibilities under Jewish law. The bride and groom do not see one another until the **b'deken,** or veiling of the bride. The groom is led into the room where the bride and both mothers, along with the women, surround the bride. The groom lowers the veil over the bride's face indicating he is only interested in her inner beauty. This ceremony is based on the story of Jacob as he was tricked into marrying the sister of his beloved Rachel.

The **huppah** is the canopy under which Jewish couples are married. It dates back to the time when the Hebrews were nomadic people in the desert and only under a canopy was there a cool and intimate place for shelter from the elements. When the couple enters the huppah, the bride circles the groom seven times representing seven wedding blessings and the seven days of creation. Having the groom in the center is interpreted to mean that he is at the center of her world. The **kiddushin** is the actual wedding ceremony and takes place under the huppah. It begins with a blessing and a sip of wine, and a recitation of an ancient Aramaic phrase as the groom places the wedding ring on the bride's finger, believed to be the finger directly connected to the bride's heart.

The **sheva b'rachot,** are the seven blessings which are composed of praise for God, a prayer for peace for Jerusalem, and blessings for the couple. The **Breaking of the Glass** represents the fragility of life and serves as a reminder that marriage changes the lives of those married forever. It's the official signal for everyone to shout, "Mazel Tov," which means to let the celebration begin. The **yihud** is a brief time after all the hustle and bustle surrounding the wedding for the bride and groom to retreat into a private room for personal time where no one else is allowed to go. They are there alone simply to share a few moments with one another.[19]

Groom's Interfaith Marriage Assessment

(Practical Concerns for Christian — Jewish Marriages)

The following questionnaire is intended to reflect your feelings on issues surrounding your upcoming interfaith Jewish/Christian marriage. Please take a moment to fill out the requested responses, being as honest as possible regarding the concerns addressed. Remember, your responses will enable the pastor to bring focus in your next session to the concerns you have listed.

1. Have you and your fiancée discussed any of the concerns that might be involved in your upcoming interfaith marriage? What are some of the concerns you have thought about?

_____

_____

2. Are there things about your fiancée's religious tradition that concern you? _____

_____

3. Do you feel there are things about your religious tradition that concern your fiancée? _____

_____

_____

4. How do you and your fiancée expect to handle the differences between your religious traditions?

_____

_____

5. Are there things about your fiancée's religious heritage that you do not understand? _____

_____

_____

6. What are some of the striking differences between your two religious traditions? _____

_____

_____

7. How do you feel the two separate traditions will affect your marriage? _____

_____

8. Would you say you are:

      a. _____ Highly committed to your religious heritage, practices, and beliefs.

      b. _____ Nominally committed.

      c. _____ My religious heritage is not so important.

9. How concerned is your family that you are entering an interfaith marriage?

      a. _____ My family is very concerned.

      b. _____ My family accepts the marriage with reservation.

      c. _____ It doesn't matter at all.

10. Have you and your fiancée talked about having children and in which faith tradition the children would be raised?

_____

_____

11. In terms of customs and traditions in your fiancée's heritage, how comfortable do you feel?

_____

T for True — F for False

_____ I feel very comfortable around my fiancée's family.

_____ My fiancée and I feel very comfortable with all aspects of our interfaith marriage.

_____ My fiancée and I are comfortable with the plans we have made regarding handling our religious differences.

Bride's Interfaith Marriage Assessment

(Practical Concerns for Christian — Jewish Marriages)

The following questionnaire is intended to reflect your feelings on issues surrounding your upcoming interfaith Jewish/Christian marriage. Please take a moment to fill out the requested responses, being as honest as possible regarding the concerns addressed. Remember, your responses will enable the pastor to bring focus in your next session to the concerns you have listed.

1. Have you and your fiancé discussed any of the concerns that might be involved in your upcoming interfaith marriage? What are some of the concerns you have thought about?

_____

_____

2. Are there things about your fiancé's religious tradition that concern you? _____

_____

3. Do you feel there are things about your religious tradition that concern your fiancé? _____

_____

_____

4. How do you and your fiancé expect to handle the differences between your religious traditions?

_____

_____

5. Are there things about your fiancé's religious heritage that you do not understand? _____

_____

_____

6. What are some of the striking differences between your two religious traditions? _____

_____

_____

7. How do you feel the two separate traditions will affect your marriage? _____

_____

8. Would you say you are:

    a. _____ Highly committed to your religious heritage, practices, and beliefs.

    b. _____ Nominally committed.

    c. _____ My religious heritage is not so important.

9. How concerned is your family that you are entering an interfaith marriage?

    a. _____ My family is very concerned.

    b. _____ My family accepts the marriage with reservation.

    c. _____ It doesn't matter at all.

10. Have you and your fiancé talked about having children and in which faith tradition the children would be raised?

_____

_____

11. In terms of customs and traditions in your fiancé's heritage, how comfortable do you feel?

_____

T for True — F for False

_____ I feel very comfortable around my fiancé's family.

_____ My fiancé and I feel very comfortable with all aspects of our interfaith marriage.

_____ My fiancé and I are comfortable with the plans we have made regarding handling our religious differences.

Black — White Marriages

The interfacing of people that began in nursery school and continued through high school and college has had its effect on interracial marriages as the number of interracial marriages continues to increase, although not at the rate one might expect. Since 1970 the number of black-white couples marrying has increased by more than 400 %. The number of interracial marriages in 1970 was 65,000. In 1996, it was 296,000. Chances are the percentages of increase will continue to rise as the mixing of America continues.[20]

In reflecting on interracial marriages, David Shipler concluded that men and women who marry across racial lines do not see their action as heroic. Like others who marry, these couples meet, fall in love, and marry with eyes mostly wide open, looking to find meaning and happiness in their relationship and hoping to navigate their children through the troubled waters of identity.[21]

The issue of race does not disappear from black — white marriages after the day of the wedding, but continues to be a sleeper in the exchange of human interaction within the household. Generally, interracial marriages work best when each partner sees the other as a human being first, and then as a white human being or black human being with all the cultural and historical ingredients that come with membership in the larger group.

Couples who try to leave the issue of race at the front doorstep will usually discover that society has a way of pushing it inside, even if they would rather that it remain outside. In the end, biracial children will bring the issue front and center. Successful interracial marriages are usually those who tackle whatever discussion head-on, and those whose affection embraces the whole person including the more apparent characteristic, that of one's race.

Those who marry across racial lines are usually already comfortable with each other's cultures. Blacks have usually attained an easy biculturalism and feel at ease in white environments. Whites have usually spent enough time in black cultures to feel relaxed, but once married, may experience a crash course in racism.

The most painful intolerance a couple may face is from their own nuclear and extended family. Such bigotry can force a couple to visit relatives solo or pressure children to leave a parent behind when a visit is made to a grandparent's home. The initial chilling effect may thaw, but the residual emotions may linger for extended periods and may, in fact, never totally disappear.

Scales that measure social distance between one race and another have invariably found that the relationship that triggers the strongest feelings of ethnocentricity is marriage. Sociologists have found that white Americans have tolerating attitudes toward having blacks in jobs, in their neighborhoods, and at their children's schools, but resistance to intermarriage remains strong. One study found that two-thirds of the sample surveyed declared they would disapprove of a close relative marrying a black.[22]

Biracial couples may experience subliminal racial anxieties in the marriage, anxieties that are present, but may or may not ever surface. Black spouses may wonder how they are viewed by their white partners and white spouses may fight against ingrained prejudices. If prejudice is well engrained, they may have to work to overcome the silent voices inside.

Concomitant with marrying across racial lines is the concern for bridging the cultural gap that may exist between whites and blacks on any number of issues. Child-rearing practices, dialect,

159

music, and worship styles are but a few cultural differences that may be pronounced. Sometimes it is difficult to determine whether certain differences are, in fact, racial differences, or cultural differences that have developed over periods of time as races have been segregated into separate cultural traditions. Both black and white cultures have subcultures within their larger cultures. Subcultures usually organize themselves around class, region, religion, and ethnicity. Italian Americans are quite different from WASP Episcopalians, but all white cultures do meet some common ground which is called "Anglo culture." Black cultures also possess regional and social distinctions. The southern rural black would perceive life quite differently from the northern urban black.[23]

Moving between white and black cultures may also note differences in language and dress styles. There is a "white English," and a "black English." There is a "white attire" and a "black attire," and most blacks can easily move between both the language and dress boundaries, while whites have difficulty adapting to either the language or the dress structures. When black dialects creep into white speech, it is sometimes met with resistance. Differences can also come in subtle forms. Many blacks see their culture as exhibiting an inventiveness to humor, close family ties, honesty in friendship, spontaneity of expression of feeling, and dignity in struggle.[24]

The issues of interracial marriage are complex and numerous. Overcoming the numerous impediments that surround marrying across the color line is challenging for both whites and blacks. Yet, as was said in the introduction to this session on Mixed Marriages, love has the quality of transcending all other virtues and values, customs and traditions. It does "bear all things, believe all things, hope all things, and endure all things." At times disapproval and resistance in whatever form and from whatever party have to take a backseat to this the greatest of virtues, and two people from different races, cultures, and traditions fall in love and are willing to take the leap of faith with the desire to confirm their love in the solemn setting of marriage in their place of faith and worship. Hence, they come to their spiritual leader and guide, their pastor, for his/her guidance and the church's blessing.

The following assessment will enable prospective black — white couples planning to be married to process their perspectives, feelings, and evaluations regarding their mixed marriage. The couple will have already talked about a number of related subjects, but in all probability not processed their feelings in an in-depth way. The assessment instrument will force the couple to address many of the questions surrounding an interracial marriage.

160

Groom's Interracial Marriage Assessment

(Bridging Racial and Cultural Barriers for Success in Interracial Marriage)

The purpose of this survey is for you to reflect on the issues surrounding your upcoming interracial marriage in order for you to process your thoughts and to be able to conceptualize the meanings of those concerns as they may come into play for your marriage, extended family, children, and community. Please take a moment to fill out the responses, being as honest and forthright as you can be. Remember, your responses will enable the pastor to bring focus in your next session to the concerns you have listed.

1. Have you and your fiancée talked through any of the concerns that might be involved in your upcoming interracial marriage? What are some of the issues that seem most pronounced/important?

_____

_____

2. Have you discussed the implications of an interracial marriage

   a. _____ A great deal?

   b. _____ Somewhat?

   c. _____ Hardly at all?

3. Are there some things about your proposed marriage that give you particular anxiety/concern/worry?

_____

_____

4. Have you discussed your upcoming marriage with your family, and if so, how did they feel about it?

   _____ Yes, I have discussed it.

   _____ No, I have not discussed it.

Family's response of support or nonsupport: _____

5. What problems, if any, do you foresee in your upcoming marriage with regards to its being an interracial marriage?

_____

_____

6. Do you feel there are similarities between your cultural heritages? _____

_____

7. Are there striking differences between your cultural heritage and that of your fiancée?

_____

8. How do you feel when you visit with your fiancée's family? _____

_____

9. How do you think your fiancée feels when she visits with your family? _____

_____

10. Are you aware of any resistance to your upcoming marriage? _____

_____

11. How is your fiancee's family different from yours? _____

_____

12. How is it similar to yours? _____

13. What is your comfort level when you are visiting in your fiancée's home, church, or community?

_____ Very comfortable

_____ Somewhat comfortable

_____ Ill at ease

14. Have you noted any differences between your heritage and that of your fiancée with regards to:

    a. _____ Music Preferences

    b. _____ Worship Styles

    c. _____ Dialect

    d. _____ Family Traditions

    e. _____ Preferred Dress/attire

    f. _____ Cultural Heritage

    g. _____ Child Rearing Practices

15. If differences have been noted in the preceding question, how have you addressed those differences?

_____

16. How confident do you feel that you and your fiancée will be able to surmount the obstacles that may stand in the way of an interracial marriage?

_____ Very confident

_____ Confident

_____ Would like a greater sense of confidence

17. Do you plan to have children? _____

18. What measures do you think you will have to take in order for your child(ren) to become adjusted to the veracity of the biracial world in which they shall live?

_____

T for True — F for False

_____ My fiancée and I have thoroughly talked through our upcoming interracial marriage.

_____ Both our families are comfortable with our upcoming mixed marriage.

_____ We understand there may be resistance to our marriage, but are willing to surmount whatever resistance we may encounter.

_____ We look forward to having children and are prepared to enable our children to overcome whatever obstacles they may encounter from being racially mixed children.

_____ We understand our fiancée's cultural heritage may be different from ours, but will do our best to appreciate her traditions and cultural values.

_____ We believe the joy of being married outweighs the obstacles we may encounter in having an interracial marriage.

_____ We have discussed all the ramifications of this marriage and feel comfortable in the decision we are making to be married.

_____ We see no problem areas in the upcoming marriage.

Bride's Interracial Marriage Assessment

(Bridging Racial and Cultural Barriers for Success in Interracial Marriage)

The purpose of this survey is for you to reflect on the issues surrounding your upcoming interracial marriage in order for you to process your thoughts and to be able to conceptualize the meanings of those concerns as they may come into play for your marriage, extended family, children, and community. Please take a moment to fill out the responses, being as honest and forthright as you can be. Remember, your responses will enable the pastor to bring focus in your next session to the concerns you have listed.

1. Have you and your fiancé talked through any of the concerns that might be involved in your upcoming interracial marriage? What are some of the issues that seem most pronounced/important?

_____

_____

2. Have you discussed the implications of an interracial marriage

    a. _____ A great deal?

    b. _____ Somewhat?

    c. _____ Hardly at all?

3. Are there some things about your proposed marriage that give you particular anxiety/concern/worry?

_____

_____

4. Have you discussed your upcoming marriage with your family, and if so, how did they feel about it?

_____ Yes, I have discussed it.

_____ No, I have not discussed it.

Family's response of support or nonsupport: _____

5. What problems, if any, do you foresee in your upcoming marriage with regards to its being an interracial marriage?

_____

_____

6. Do you feel there are similarities between your cultural heritages? _____

_____

7. Are there striking differences between your cultural heritage and that of your fiancé?

_____

8. How do you feel when you visit with your fiancé's family? _____

_____

9. How do you think your fiancé feels when he visits with your family? _____

_____

10. Are you aware of any resistance to your upcoming marriage? _____

_____

11. How is your fiancé's family different from yours? _____

_____

12. How is it similar to yours? _____

13. What is your comfort level when you are visiting in your fiancé's home, church, or community?

_____ Very comfortable

_____ Somewhat comfortable

_____ Ill at ease

14. Have you noted any differences between your heritage and that of your fiancé with regards to:

    a. _____ Music Preferences

    b. _____ Worship Styles

    c. _____ Dialect

    d. _____ Family Traditions

    e. _____ Preferred Dress/attire

    f. _____ Cultural Heritage

    g. _____ Child Rearing Practices

15. If differences have been noted in the preceding question, how have you addressed those differences?

_____

16. How confident do you feel that you and your fiancé will be able to surmount the obstacles that may stand in the way of an interracial marriage?

_____ Very confident

_____ Confident

_____ Would like a greater sense of confidence

17. Do you plan to have children? _____

18. What measures do you think you will have to take in order for your child(ren) to become adjusted to the veracity of the biracial world in which they shall live?

_____

T for True — F for False

_____ My fiancé and I have thoroughly talked through our upcoming interracial marriage.

_____ Both our families are comfortable with our upcoming mixed marriage.

_____ We understand there may be resistance to our marriage, but are willing to surmount whatever resistance we may encounter.

_____ We look forward to having children and are prepared to enable our children to overcome whatever obstacles they may encounter from being racially mixed children.

_____ We understand our fiancé's cultural heritage may be different from ours, but will do our best to appreciate her traditions and cultural values.

_____ We believe the joy of being married outweighs the obstacles we may encounter in having an interracial marriage.

_____ We have discussed all the ramifications of this marriage and feel comfortable in the decision we are making to be married.

_____ We see no problem areas in the upcoming marriage.

Concluding the Session

The mixed marriage session should be concluded by reviewing the key points of the marriage, whether it is an interfaith marriage or a racially mixed marriage. The pastor should ask the couple if there are any areas of concern regarding the interfaith or mixed marriage that were not covered which the couple would like to have addressed or if any questions remain. The pastor should inform the couple that the next session will focus on the marriage service itself. The pastor may close the session with a prayer reflective of interfaith or mixed marriages.

Sample Closing Prayers

Holy God, you are far more mindful than we of the things that separate us one from another and the things that bring us together. Here are N_____ and N_____ whose different faith traditions have separated so many one from another, but whose love and commitment to one another are able to transcend even those differences. It is said that marriages are made in heaven, and just now reflecting upon all the hurdles that have been and are yet to be overcome, we understand that only through the gift of heaven itself could this love find fruition and favor, and yet here we see this love blossoming and coming into full flower. We thank you for love that is stronger than all that separates. Bless these dear ones that in the home they are to establish, you will be the ever unseen, but present guest. Amen.

God of the ages, you have revealed yourself in such mysteries. It seems we have compartmentalized you in the ways we know and worship you, yet you are the same God in whom we live and move and have our being. As we contemplate this upcoming marriage from such diverse traditions, enable us to understand that you are always the same God; it is we who experience you in such different dimensions. We know there are those who place great importance on concepts about you. Yet, we also understand how love is able to conquer all things, even the fervor of feeling which is the dynamic that is central in the faith of those whose lives we are a part. Bless N_____ and N_____ in the love they have found in one another and enable them to understand how love truly bears, believes, endures, and hopes all things. Amen.

Lord, more than anyone else, you understood how differences were able to divide and even destroy people. When you walked on earth, you saw division everywhere: Jew and Roman, publican and Pharisee, and Jew and Samaritan. Yet your prayer was that "all may be one, even as you and your heavenly Father are one." Here are N_____ and N_____ whose traditions separate them, but whose love unites them. Bless that love that it may overcome every wall of separation. In your name, we pray. Amen.

Optional Session II

Second Marriages

(Helping Couples Embrace a Positive Future)

People who have been married once usually want to be married again. The percentage of people who express no desire to be married again after having been married once is fairly small. Those who were once married found fulfillment in the institution of marriage through needs fulfillment, companionship, or the need to affiliate, even if their marriage ended in a separation and divorce. Marriages end either due to the death of a spouse or due to separation and divorce. In either case, there is pain and the need for healing and repairing the brokenness that is encountered. Being a widow or widower is quite different from the intentional ending of a marriage, but even marriages that are intentionally ended experience stages of grief, and in fact, some stages may be amplified because in addition to loss, one may also be dealing with rejection. Either form of ending a marriage has its own set of distresses and before a person is ready to move into another relationship, those concerns must be addressed and emotionally processed. Before addressing the subject of marriage after widowhood, let us explore some of the issues that surround marriage after divorce.

Separation and divorce are a fact of the twenty-first century, whether we want to admit it or not. While the church would like to think that every marriage will succeed and the married couple will live happily ever after, statistics do not bear this out to be the case. Separations and divorce were rapidly on the rise in the last quarter of the twentieth century and only recently has there been the slightest reversal of that trend. It is quite startling that one out of two marriages will end in divorce. While statistics are cold, every separation and divorce means there is deep hurt in the lives of those who are ending their marriage and the dreams which led them to the altar now stand in ashes.

There are many divergent opinions and positions regarding marriage after divorce and the church's proper role. The most pronounced difference is between Catholics and Protestants, since marriage is revered as one of the seven sacraments in the Catholic Church, while in the Protestant, though not a sacrament, nonetheless it is a most sacred union, blessed by the church and honored by God. Within Protestantism there is a wide spectrum of opinion regarding what role the church should play in offering its blessings in marrying those who are divorced.

Every pastor should be knowledgeable of his/her church's position. It is not difficult to find that information, as it is printed in most books of church discipline or church order. If it is not so readily available in print, a call to the judicatory or headquarters of the church will bring forth an answer regarding the position a particular denomination may hold. Not only is it incumbent on the pastor to understand the larger church's position, it is also necessary for the pastor to arrive at some conclusion/position concerning his/her own thoughts, for surely every pastor will be approached to marry persons who have been married before and whose marriage ended in divorce. It is not a matter of *if* the pastor will be asked, but *when*. Working through one's own position, as well as being knowledgeable of the position of one's church, will provide the groundwork for responding to couples who have been divorced and wish to be married again with the blessings of the church.

The definition of divorce is the legal dissolution of marriage. It has been a concern of the Judeo-Christian tradition since the early history of Israel. In the Book of Deuteronomy 24:1-4, it is stated that Moses tolerated divorce if a man found some indecency with his wife. The divorce was finalized when the wife was granted a written statement of release and sent out of the house. Mosaic law was, of course, founded within a patriarchal society where men had the upper hand. No mention was made regarding what might happen if a wife found her husband to be indecent.

The school of Shammah that existed just prior to the time of Christ, and a school of thought with which Christ was no doubt familiar, taught that a man could not lawfully be divorced from his wife unless he found her guilty of some action that was really infamous and contrary to the rules of virtue. The Pharisees attempted to trap Jesus into some statement with which they could take issue, but he declined to interpret Moses' words, though he declared that he regarded all the lesser causes than unfaithfulness as standing on ground too weak to grant such a certificate.

Much church law and understanding is based on Jesus' words from the Sermon on the Mount found in Matthew 5:31-33. The passage reads as follows:

> *"It is also said, 'Whoever divorces his wife, let him give her a certificate of divorce.' But I say to you that every one who divorces his wife, except on the ground of unchastity, makes her an adulteress; and whoever marries a divorced woman commits adultery."*

In the twenty-first century world when the church is surrounded by and often made up of people who are in their second and even third marriages, how is the church to respond in faithfulness to Jesus' teachings and, at the same time, respond to the realities of the world? One solution embraced by many churches and pastors is not to offer the church's blessings to second marriages, but to invite the couples to affirm their vows before a civil magistrate. The church may offer counseling before and after, but reserve the right not to bless the marriage before the altar of God. Churches that take this position usually have within their ranks numerous couples who are in their second and third marriages.

The ministry of the church is to embrace these couples and their blended families, minister to their spiritual needs, and assimilate them into the life of the congregation. Certainly, the church wants to turn its back on no one, for it is in every way a hospital for sinners and not a home for saints.

Other churches and pastors feel that divorce and remarriage is simply dealing with the realities of the times, and the church should reach out to couples whose lives have gone asunder in their attempt at marriage and family. They believe God is a God of second chances and that the church's mission is one of grace. This approach holds that there may have been real reasons why the first marriage did not work out and that it should be the position of the church to be a compassionate enabler in the hope and faith that the new relationship is built upon a more solid foundation and mature judgment than the first.

If it is the position of the pastor to marry those who have been married before and for whatever reason found it best to end that marriage, care should be given to guide the couple spiritually in their thinking and journey toward remarriage and the establishment of their new home and family. There are even greater considerations now than the first time around, and all of those issues need to be addressed carefully and resolved in order that the trials and mistakes of the first marriage not filter into the second. There is a need to review the first marriage and enable couples to understand

172

and come to terms with what went wrong and why the marriage did not succeed. Only by understanding and addressing those issues will couples be ready to move on into their new relationship and leave the old behind.

Commensurate with the concern of marriage after divorce is the question and issue of children from the former marriage. If there are children, whether children in custody or children with visitation rights, it is not simply a matter of joining two lives, but joining two families. Children have feelings and loyalties to their birth parents and often blame themselves for the marriage not having worked. Children go to extreme measures to keep their moms and dads together and may experience various stages of the grief from denial, to bargaining, to anger, with final acceptance coming, if at all, long after every other stage has long since past.

Children are often left with feelings of resentment, either subliminal or openly expressed. They may conclude that their feelings and overtures to save their parents' marriage were ignored or that they simply did not count. They may feel dragged into the new marriage kicking and screaming and powerless to counter decisions made by the remarrying parent. Issues such as giving up their former residence, friends, school, community, home, and room may be sources of anger and resentment.

Blending siblings from two former marriages into one household also has its challenges. Children may react to the new family setting by forming coalitions with the siblings of their birth family and holding the siblings of their new family at bay. An only child from one former marriage may feel outnumbered and overwhelmed by two or more siblings in the new marriage and family. They may perceive favoritism, whether real or imagined.

While every second marriage or blended family will not be besieged by such feelings from children, and some will in fact welcome a new household where there is love, acceptance, affirmation, peace, and harmony, couples with children considering a second marriage should be cognizant of the many facets of emotions entering a second marriage may generate within the minds and hearts of their children.

Children deal with their emotions in a number of ways. Some react with open aggression and expressions of anger. Others react with prolonged passive aggression, not speaking, withdrawing, sulking, staying in their rooms, displaying antisocial behavior, or being negative toward the people they feel have caused the pain in their lives.

Couples need to process the many issues surrounding blended families carefully. They need to involve the children in open discussions regarding the possibility of remarriage and a new family and how they might feel about it. Giving children the opportunity to talk and honestly be listened to and understood will enable them to process their emotions, deal with their losses, and anticipate hope and joy in their lives after the experiences of transition.

In the process of preparing couples for marriages after divorce in which in-house children will be involved, pastors may wish to invite the children to a session and allow them the opportunity to talk through some of their feelings. Here the pastor stands in a unique position not only to enable children to process their feelings, but to facilitate perspectives of understanding and support for parents who are also processing their own feelings as well as seeking to be supportive of their children.

One opportunity to enable children to process their feelings is to involve them in the planning of the wedding and to invite them to participate in the service and the surrounding celebrations. Some wedding services have sections of the service that recognize the presence of children from previous marriages and formally seek their love and support for the present marriage (see, for instance, "Services of Marriage," *The Book of Worship, United Church of Christ*). If children do not endorse the marriage, it is still better for them to be involved than ignored or circumvented. The watchword for parents and the pastor is *sensitivity*. Being sensitive to feelings goes a long ways toward healing and even acceptance.

Getting married after the death of a spouse brings a whole different set of emotions and circumstances. There is no doctrinal reason from the church's position why someone whose spouse has died may not be married again. The remarrying person fulfilled his/her marital vows, as it was the death of the spouse that ended the marriage and not an intentional action on the part of the person.

Widowed persons approach remarriage not only from a different set of emotions, but often from an entirely different perspective. Such persons are not dealing so much with any sense of failure or rejection, as they are loss and grief. They are not asking why something did not work, but processing their emotions of why such pain was thrust upon them or why their spouse suffered in the way they may have suffered.

Widowed persons may have reacted to their loss by putting the idea of remarriage on the table for an extended period of time, thinking they may never be married again because no one could ever take the place of the one they lost. They may feel it is an affront to their deceased spouse to remarry, that it shows lack of love or lack of respect. The hurt of their grief may have cut so deeply, they may be reluctant to expose themselves to the vulnerability of the pain of another loss.

The flip side of grief for widowed people is the need to have someone in their life to fill the hurt and emptiness. Losing a spouse leaves a gaping hole and an empty heart, and without the presence of another, life can be very lonely and difficult. Some people simply have to have someone in their lives to feel a sense of completeness, or to fill the void, or to offer support and encouragement. Such personalities cannot make it alone and the loss of their spouse only amplifies their need and loneliness.

Time is also a factor for widowed persons. First and foremost is the question of the amount of time required for healing. That process can take months and years, even scores of years. For some, the loss is too great and life is too short and there is not enough time to heal the brokenness they feel. For others, the healing process is accelerated as they are able to process their loss and look hopefully to rebuilding their life in the future.

The passage of time is also related to social expectations regarding one's re-entry into a relationship following the death of a spouse. How much time is the right amount of time is the question that is often internally considered, though seldom verbalized. For the surviving spouse who may want another relationship, it is a matter of the amount of time required for the healing process as well as feeling social pressure in the form of encouragement to find another relationship or shame for even thinking such thoughts so soon after their spouse's death. For children who feel that no one else could ever take Mom or Dad's place, there may never enough time. Middle-aged widowed persons who may be considering remarriage after the death of a spouse may feel they have all the time in the world as there is no need to hurry. Elderly people who wish to remarry feel time is of the essence, realizing their married time together is limited, perhaps counted more in terms of months than years.

Children play a special role in the decision of widowed persons to remarry. Young widows/widowers may be left with the responsibility of young children and have a special need for love and support. Widows/widowers of teenage children may find their children processing the loss of their parent rather quickly and reengaging themselves with their peers and activities, unaware or insensitive to the pain and sorrow going on inside their mom or dad. Widowed persons of older children may find their children far too engaged in their own lives to be concerned with the grief of their parent. Children react differently to the issue of Mom or Dad remarrying after the death of their other parent. Some children feel a sense of ownership of their parents and resent any one coming in to take the place of the mom or dad that died. Other children see the remaining parent as lonely and needful of support and companionship and welcome the opportunity for that parent to find someone in his or her life.

But people do move on into new relationships after they have suffered such great losses and grief experiences in their lives. Processing the new relationship is often as important for children as it is for those remarrying, and sensitivity on the part of parents can avoid a lot of pitfalls, resentment, and deep hurt.

There are a number of positive steps parents may take to enable children to process the new marriage and form relationships within the new family. It is important to be proactive in making conscious efforts for allowing the child to see that the new parent is committed to the new relationship and that it has all the possibilities of being a good one not only for his/her parent who is remarrying, but there are possibilities for the child as well. Enabling the child to see opportunities for love, companionship, and security in the new family will allow hope and anticipation to replace feelings of loss, gloom, and negativity. The following suggestions may serve as proactive tools for parents in building bridges to children coming into a blended family, even if the blended family is the result of the death of a spouse and parent.

Twenty Pro-Active Suggestions for
Bridge Building in Blended Families

1. **Be Positive about the Parent from the Former Marriage.** Children are a part of and an extension of their family and parents, and as such they will rise to the defense of their parents even in cases in which there has been abuse, mistreatment, or neglect. In such cases, children may accept the fact that there has been abuse, but their parents are still their parents, and children feel the need to love and honor them and defend them, if it is perceived that parents are under attack. The parent/child bond was created early in life when parents were the significant and powerful other on which the child depended for life and security. It is a strong bond and one that outlasts and transcends opposition or compelling intrusions.

   It would be unwise and even reckless for a stepparent to try to win approval at the expense of the birth parent from the former marriage. Being critical of the parent is perceived as being critical of the child himself/herself and the reaction would be what could only be expected: defensiveness, and more to overcome in terms of reaching out to the child.

   The new parent from the blended family marriage should look for opportunities to build up the parent from the former marriage. Being positive will not only win the heart of the child, it will show him/her that there is nothing to fear from the new parent and that he/she is a team player for the welfare of the child and the entire family. This will build powerfully positive feelings within the child, in addition to building his/her self-esteem.

2. **Anticipate a Wonderful Future.** In concert with the child, intentional conversations should be held regarding the wonderful possibilities that lie ahead. Allow the child to see that the new family will be doing fun and exciting things together and that he/she will be a part of it all. Share with the child that plans are already in place and implement some of those plans before the marriage actually takes place. Have conversations about the new home, new school, and all the new friends that are just waiting. Help the child to see a future for himself/herself, that life will go on, and that there are wonderful possibilities looming for his/her participation. If there is to be a move, take the child to see the new home and surroundings so that all guesswork is taken away and judgments are made on sound facts. Promises should never be made that cannot and will not be fulfilled, as such would only be another disappointment and would breach the trust one is so desperately seeking to establish.

3. **Give More Than Is Necessary.** Blending families is an emotional experience in every sense of the word. It is a time of transition, of leaving a past and familiarity, and stepping into an unknown future. During such a time, emotions are fragile and nerves are raw. Life seems open-ended with a flavor of uncertainty. People are more vulnerable. Such conditions are not a time for restraint when it comes to giving and affirming. Parents need to understand the forces that have come to bear in their children's lives and respond in a spirit of giving more than even seems necessary in terms of the needs of their children.

4. **Find Reasons to Thank the Child.** Recognition is a human need. Everyone likes to be recognized or thanked for deeds well done. In the course of a day any member of a family may do a number of things worthy of appreciation, which is nothing more than recognition. As a

rule, people respond quite positively to those who have taken the time to take note of the good that has been done. A grateful attitude is therefore a winning attitude. Gratitude has the power to transcend many walls of resistance because it so succinctly zeros in to the heart and this most basic of human needs.

5. **Tell Jokes, Laugh Together.** Laughter has a way of breaking down walls. It can call a truce even between enemies. Children are noticeably given to laughter and are able to see humor in places often overlooked by adults. Children can laugh on a pin drop, and things that seem funny to kids seem silly or are often overlooked by adults. Each succeeding generation of kids has its own set of children's jokes that seem awfully funny to those kids, but unscrutable in terms of humor to others. The "knock-knock" jokes seemed to have hung around for a long time, but even they seem to be passing from the scene as new children's humor becomes the fad. But jokes don't have to be in vogue for children to laugh. They understand humor and will laugh at most anything that is remotely funny. They will even laugh at the person trying to be funny when he comes across as not so funny. They think trying to be funny is funny. Children love to laugh and laughter can be the gateway to the heart of a child.

6. **Create and Maintain Secrets.** Secrets are privileged information shared by only those most trusted and those closest to us. We never share private information with those whom we perceive to be in opposition, as that would violate our sense of propriety, or with those who may use that information against us. By telling a secret, we are taking someone into our confidence and are sending a message that we trust that person with very private information. Like the rest of us, children like to feel they are included in the inner circle when covert information is being shared and they feel honored they are trusted enough to be a confidant. Secrets can be real bridge builders in the arena of blending families.

7. **Go on an Outing Together.** Time spent with children is never time wasted. The simple act of inviting a child on an outing to a movie, a park, the beach, a picnic, a ball game, shopping, the circus, the zoo, a parade, or any activity where there is quality time with the child may overcome a deadlock and soften the relationship so that there is a feeling of common ground.

8. **Make Every Attempt to Be a Bright Spot.** Children who have lived through the experience of seeing their parents go through the pain of separation and divorce are already walking wounded and are living in the well of deep hurt. They may feel life has lost its luster and that someone has let the air out of their balloon. They may blame themselves for the way things turned out and run the "what if" tapes over and over. Regardless of how things may look on the surface, things may be rather dark on the inside and any ray of sunshine would be a welcomed bright spot. What children do not need is for someone to rain on their parade. What they do need are smiles, joy, and enthusiasm to help them through the season of emotional decompression into the brighter days of rainbows, sunshine, and dreams.

9. **Practice Giving Praise.** Praise works wonders. Praise changes moods. Praise tears down walls. Praise builds bridges. Praise brightens days and lightens loads. Praise builds self-worth. Praise touches the heart. Praise boosts morale. Praise pushes forward. Praise endears and

embraces. Praise makes one feel worthy. Praise is a spirit lifter and a people builder. Praise focuses on the positive. Praise looks for opportunities. Praise endorses. Praise is the lighter of candles. Praise can mend a broken heart.

10. **Be a Friend.** "A friend is a gift you give yourself," so the saying goes. Who better to have as a friend than a child? Children are lovable, affable, pleasant, and usually agreeable. They reach out to those who show they care. It's fun being around a child because in his/her innocence, so much can be given. The old adage, "A friend in need is a friend indeed," could never be more accurately spoken than when referring to a child who has experienced the disintegration of his former family. Such is a time when a child needs a friend. Becoming a friend is an opportunity to reach across a chasm, embrace a child's heart, and open a door to the future.

11. **Believe in the Power of Love.** The Apostle Paul was intuitive and discerning when he put his thoughts to pen in his 13th Chapter of Corinthians. Applying his words to the efforts of blending a family addresses the power of love to overcome and conquer the walls of resistance and mend hearts that are broken. Family transition is a time when emotions are tender and feelings easily bruised. Paul's words could not be more fitting, and parents wishing to build bridges in merging families should take note: *"Love is patient and kind; love is not jealous or boastful; it is not arrogant or rude. Love does not insist on its own way; it is not irritable or resentful; it does not rejoice at the wrong, but rejoices in the right. Love bears all things, believes all things, hopes all things, endures all things. Love never ends"* (I Corinthians 13:4-8a). Love has power and love works miracles. Love never gives up.

12. **Be the Parent You Would Like to Have.** The simple act of putting ourselves in someone else's shoes changes the perspective of simply seeing that person as a fixed entity to understanding that person is a person with feelings, has highs and lows, dreams, feels hurt, delights in joy, needs support, knows loneliness, experiences moods, has aspirations, and has scores and scores of needs. When families are in transition, parents need to look at their children and ask themselves, "What is my child feeling right now?" or "If I were in his/her place, what would life be like for me?" A decision to be the kind of parent you would like to have if you were in the child's place may transform one's thinking and enable that parent to be more sensitive, caring, and present in the life of the child. This exercise should be practiced daily until one senses a transformation of his/her own perspective.

13. **Avoid Triangulation.** Triangulation is the complicated configuration of personalities in which two people in a triad are in union to the exclusion of the third. Triangulation is a common occurrence in three-way relationships where there is occasion for two people to coalesce, thus isolating the third. There are times when it is appropriate and expected and times when it is dangerous. In terms of parental guidance and discipline, it would be expected that the two parents would maintain unanimity in their disciplining overtures toward the child. Sending the same signal from both parents sends the message the child is the "third party," and it is incumbent on him to correct his behavior. But in terms of ongoing familial interaction, no one wants to be left out or to feel like a third party. No where is this more able to be seen than in the blending of families when a child from a former marriage is cast into the setting of a new

178

family in which he/she perceives himself/herself as a third party. Every effort should be made to avoid triangulation and every effort made to include the child in every opportunity of involvement in the new family.

14. **Be Flexible.** The process of blending families is infused with all kinds of knee-jerk reactions associated with merging and assimilating personalities involved in pervious family relationships into new family relationships. Baggage from the past does drag emotions into the present, emotions that may be tender or volatile. Emotional transference often conceals the true sources of pain, estrangement, or underlying sentiment. Such times are not times for rigid approaches, as inflexibility only immobilizes emotional expression and often sets feelings in concrete. On the other hand, flexibility gives needed space for sharing what is in one's heart and soul, as there is an atmosphere of openness and affirmation. Simply having space in which to maneuver emotionally can, in itself, be oil for troubled waters and balm for healing. In the process of building and growing new families from previous or existing ones, the need for flexibility cannot be overstated, and the adults who are responsible for shaping the future need to be especially sensitive to parameters as they exist.

15. **Play Age-Appropriate Games.** Most every child enjoys playing games, especially if he/she is able to capture the attention of an adult either as a partner or as an opponent. Nothing thrills a child like thinking he/she has won a game over an adult opponent. One can usually observe the glee of winning in a child's eyes. As cognitive skills develop, the desire for more sophisticated and mentally challenging games also increases. Games provide unique opportunities for adults to interplay with children, opportunities that parents who are meshing two families can ill-afford to miss. Younger children usually always love Uno because they understand it and can fairly compete. Older children love Twister, Sorry, Monopoly, Trivial Pursuit, Battleship, and Operation.

16. **Look for Common Interests.** There are activities/interests which adults and children may have in common, things which they can do together to build harmony and accord. Sporting activities, while not limited to males, can usually provide common ground among men and boys. Such concerns as pulling for a favorite team, collecting their logos, watching or attending their games, keeping up with the stats, knowing who their players are, all have the potential for building bridges and cementing relationships. Shopping, beauty shops, fashion, and cosmetics are girl things, enjoyed by adults and youth alike. Massaging such interests creates feeling of inclusion and acceptance and they are great springboards to capturing hearts and winning support.

17. **Be a Cheerleader.** Cheerleaders have a unique role in the landscape of athletics. Sporting events are lackluster without someone leading the cheers. Although the focus is on the game, cheerleaders add emotion and feeling and instill team spirit, support, and stimulation to the game. Without the presence of cheerleaders gathering support and amplifying the excitement, many athletic events would be rather flat. Cheerleaders are also important in the landscape of human exchange. Everyone needs someone in his/her corner cheering them on, creating a desire to be a winner, and believing he/she is the very best. Just as athletes on the playing field

179

are buoyed by cheers and drawn toward those leading the cheers, children are also uplifted by the support of parents who lead the cheers and they are drawn toward those persons.

18. **Overcome Resistance.** Blending families is difficult even under the most favorable of circumstances. Loyalties are to familiarity, to the way it was, and often to the parent who is now absent. Children have any number of weapons at their disposal to put up a wall of resistance, and they can be quite creative and immovable in the process. In some cases, stepparents try every conceivable tactic to win over a child whose will is as steel. The temptation is to give up and throw in the towel, believing the child's heart will never be won. But perseverance always pays off and will win in the end. Stepparents who want harmony and unity must not give up; they must go the distance to overcome resistance.

19. **Include Children in Your Plans.** In planning an outing, a day's activities, or a get-away, adults often make plans to the exclusion of input from their children, assuming the things parents want to do will also be the things their children would want to do. This approach works for many families as children go along with whatever has been planned, although their own wishes have been overlooked. This approach is less plausible for stepchildren as they may already feel like the "fifth wheel" in terms of planning and inclusion. Gaining input from children creates ownership in whatever activity and should be encouraged to ensure success in bridge building in blended families.

20. **Never Give Up.** In seeking to win the hearts of a stepson/daughter, and in seeking to overcome resistance, the inclination is to give in and give up. Going on day after day, seeing very little if any sunlight, the temptation is to throw in the towel or send up the white flag. Yet surrender is not what the child wants and not what the parent wants. Mostly, children want things to be the way they were, but they know they cannot be that way again. The very strain on emotions is enough in itself to cause most to surrender. Yet, it is the NEVER GIVE UP attitude that separates winners from losers. Believing you can overcome negativity and creating a positive setting will eventually bring the much sought after victory and put the new family in the winner's circle.

After Divorce — Getting Married Again

(Profiling the Past for Success in the Future)

Everyone who marries, marries with the very best of intentions, thinking in their heart of hearts that this is the perfect union made in heaven and that they will live happily ever after. Who could imagine someone walking down the aisle thinking that if somehow this doesn't work out, it will be simple to dissolve it and move on into another marriage? No. When people marry, they believe in their heart and soul they are marrying for life and nothing will ever be able to separate them one from the other.

While those are good intentions, as they should be, the truth is that everyone who marries does not stay married. Irreconcilable differences arise. People grow at different paces and are not the same people they were when vows were exchanged. Some advance their lives through academic pursuits, while their partners remain static. The highly mobile society often places people in compromising situations where wedding vows are violated and relationships damaged beyond repair. For any number of reasons, couples may come to the conclusion that they are no longer compatible and that separation and divorce are the most viable and less painful options for everyone involved.

Separation is so painful for some people, they vow never to marry again, and have no interest whatsoever in ever pursuing another relationship. The feeling is that they gave their best, and when you get burned once, you don't put your hand on the stove simply to be burned again. Some feel they were married once and once is enough for a lifetime, that they are comfortable being single, and have no need to marry again.

There are people who have a need to be married. They love the companionship and security of married life. They yearn for the presence of another to overcome the loneliness they feel with no one around to fill the empty spaces. They conclude that just because it didn't work the first time is no reason it should not work the second time, and they are ready to move on into a new relationship.

A marriage may end and the ones married go for years and never give meeting someone else a second thought. Others may want to heal the pain of losing someone by finding another to fill the void and comfort the wounded heart. There are a thousand and one reasons why marriages fail and a thousand and one reasons why people may want to marry again. Marriage is not as flippant as dissolving one relationship and moving into another. It is a serious endeavor that reaches into the lives of many — family, friends, relatives, communities, churches, and beyond.

Any marriage that failed, failed for a reason. No one should ever consider marrying again without having clearly considered why the first marriage failed and what could be done differently in the second to ensure that the same thing did not happen again. Problem areas should be put on the table for analysis and discussion so that both people in the marriage are able to identify and process the issues, and be ready to move on into their new marriage with some sense of resolution that those issues were processed and put to rest, not to surface again.

The following inventory profiles the previous relationship, including causes for its failure, attempts at salvaging it, and corrective measures intended to ensure the success of the upcoming marriage. The inventory also addresses the concerns of children, custody, and plans to unify the new family. The inventory should be filled out by the person who has been divorced. If both the prospective bride and the groom have each been divorced, it should be filled out by both.

Profiling the Marriage That Intentionally Ended

Name of Spouse _____

Date of the First Marriage _____

Place of the First Wedding _____

Places Lived While Married _____

Education of Former Spouse _____

Occupation of Former Spouse _____

Date of Separation from Former Spouse _____

Date of Divorce _____

List the major concerns as to why the former marriage did not succeed.

1. _____

2. _____

3. _____

4. _____

Listed below are some common reasons given as to why some marriages fail. Please check the areas that you believe contributed to the failure of your first marriage:

_____ Infidelity/cheating	_____ Illness
_____ Communication	_____ Death/grief
_____ Incompatibility	_____ Differing interests
_____ Sexual problems	_____ Dissatisfaction
_____ Financial problems	_____ Financial problems
_____ In-laws	_____ Religious differences
_____ Abuse — physical or mental	_____ Self-centeredness

_____ Children   _____ Initiative

_____ Lack of support   _____ Nagging/criticism

_____ Career patterns   _____ Overspending

_____ Withholding affection   _____ Conflict

_____ Time spent at home   _____ Addictions

From the list above, was there one issue that stood out as the most important reason for your former marriage not working out?

_____

What measures did you and your former spouse take to resolve the issues in your marriage?

1. _____

2. _____

3. _____

If professional help was sought, who was the professional and how many times did you see that person?

_____

Did you think the counsel of the professional was helpful?

_____

Why do you think you were unable to salvage your relationship?

_____

What were some good points about your former marriage? _____

_____

Was the separation and divorce amiable/friendly? _____

_____

Were there attorneys involved in the dissolution of your marriage? _____

What is your relationship with your former spouse at present? _____

_____

If you had it to do over, would you do anything different in terms of enabling your former marriage to succeed?

_____

What do you feel you lost in the losing of your former marriage? _____

_____

Do you feel any sense of relief/gain now that your former marriage is behind you?

_____

How do you feel you will approach this marriage differently from your former marriage?

_____

_____

How did losing your former marriage affect your spiritual life? _____

_____

Do you feel your church has supported you through the difficulties you have experienced in your separation and divorce?

_____

Alimony

Are you paying alimony to your former spouse? _____

If you are paying alimony, have you and your fiancée/fiancé discussed the concern of alimony and is your spouse-to-be comfortable with the fact that alimony will be paid?

_____

Children and Custody

Names and Ages of Children from Former Marriage:

_____	_____
Name	Age
_____	_____
Name	Age
_____	_____
Name	Age
_____	_____
Name	Age

Who has the custody of these children? _____

_____

If you do not have custody, what are the terms of child support? _____

_____

Is your fiancée/fiancé comfortable with the child support you are rendering? _____

_____

If the children are in the custody of your former spouse, is there a possibility you will some day gain custody?

_____

Are you satisfied with the way things are regarding the custody of your children?

_____

If your children are in the custody of your former spouse, how often do you see them?

_____

Do you feel your fiancée/fiancé is satisfied with the way things are between you, your former spouse, and your children?

_____

Able to Love Again

Name of Spouse _____

Date of Marriage _____

Place of Marriage _____

Places You Lived _____

Spouse's Occupation _____

Date of Death of Spouse _____

Cause of Death _____

How did you and your spouse meet? _____

_____

What were some things that you admired most about your spouse? _____

_____

What were some of the best memories you had of her/him? _____

_____

If he/she died of an illness, was it a lingering one? _____

If he/she died in an accident, what kind of accident? _____

Who were some of the people that gave you support during the time of your grief? _____

_____

Who in particular stood out as a great resource in terms of comfort and healing? _____

_____

What was the most difficult thing about losing your wife/husband? _____

_____

How well do you think you handled losing your wife/husband? _____

_____

Below are some words that express feelings associated with grief and loss. Would you mark the ones that most aptly applied to you?

_____ Sorrow	_____ Anger
_____ Lonely	_____ Hurt
_____ Empty	_____ Guilt
_____ Bitter	_____ Disappointed
_____ Despair	_____ Immobile
_____ Insecure	_____ Disconnected
_____ At a loss	_____ Vulnerable
_____ Cheated	_____ Upended
_____ Abandoned	_____ Cut Off
_____ Fear	_____ Helpless

Select two of the words checked that most clearly describe the feelings you were experiencing in your grief and comment on the meaning of those words as they pertain to you.

Word Selected: _____ How did that word describe your grief or loss? _____

_____

Word Selected: _____ How did that word describe your grief or loss? _____

_____

It is said that time is a healer. Do you feel the passage of time has enabled you to feel any sense of healing from the loss you suffered?

_____

_____

Looking back at the loss of your wife/husband, what do you feel was the turning point in the healing process?

_____

Where is your wife/husband buried? _____

Do you ever visit the gravesite? _____

If you visit the gravesite, do you find it helpful? _____

Do you live in the same home you were living in when your wife/husband died? _____

_____

If you are living in the same home, do you plan to live there after you are remarried? _____

_____

How old were your children when your spouse died? _____

How do you feel you handled the loss of your spouse as a family? _____

_____

Do you feel the present relationship and upcoming marriage enables you to deal with the grief you have experienced?

_____

_____

Have you and you fiancée/fiancé talked about the death of your spouse and what effect it had on your life?

_____

Is your fiancée/fiancé helpful and supportive of you in your reflection on your loss and grief?

_____

Do you feel you have adequately processed your grief and are able to move on into the new marriage with strength?

_____

Blended Family Assessment

Will children be coming into your marriage from your previous marriage? _____

_____

Will children be coming into your marriage from your spouse's previous marriage? _____

_____

Has your fiancée/fiancé spent time with your children? _____

Have you spent time with your fiancée/fiancé's children? _____

How does your fiancée/fiancé get along with your children? _____

_____

How do you get along with your fiancée/fiancé's children? _____

_____

If there are children coming into the marriage from both previous marriages, do the children know each other and how do you feel they will get along?

_____

Do you foresee any problems between your fiancée/fiancé and your children? _____

_____

What have you and your fiancée/fiancée done to ensure the success of your new blended family?

_____

_____

_____

_____

Concluding the Session

This session has dealt with some very sensitive material, but it must be addressed if the prospective couple is to move forward and embrace the future with dignity, hope, and grace. The pastor ought to summarize the issues that have been addressed, focusing on the positive ways the couple intends not only to overcome the past, but also to embrace the future. Reflections given about how children will be nurtured in the forthcoming marriage should also be infused into these summary statements. The pastor may conclude the session with a prayer reflective of the issues of second marriages and blended families.

Sample Closing Prayers

You are the God of good things, O Lord, and we come before you now with grateful hearts, knowing how you continue to work wonders in our lives. You have brought N_____ and N_____ to this time and place, looking with joy and anticipation to a time of new beginnings for themselves and their lives together. You have promised that two shall be as one, and we sense that oneness in this union of kindred spirits. We shall always be thankful that you are the God of new beginnings. Bless now, these, your children, as they find in one another opportunities for wholeness and renewed commitment. Amen.

Holy God, you are the lover of souls. You are the mender of broken hearts. You are the God of every dream and every tomorrow. Just now we understand that more than ever. Surround N_____ and N_____ with love and hope. Fill their lives with rainbows, sunshine, and dreams. In our prayer time, we especially remember the children of this new home, N_____, and N_____, and N_____, that they may find in this new home a haven of blessing and a place of peace. As this new family brings together differing personalities from separate family histories and life experiences, may each be sustained and uplifted by the Spirit of him who makes all things new. Amen.

We come to you in this moment of prayer, Holy God, remembering with thanksgiving that we are held in your keeping every minute of every hour of every day. Knowing you are here gives us strength to live our lives with courage and to look to all our tomorrows with optimism and anticipation. As we look to the establishment of this new home, may N_____ and N_____ be enabled to face the future with eyes ahead and hearts wide open. May they truly understand that they are held in your keeping whether on the mountaintops or in the valleys. Enable them to hold hands in their new family circle and always to reach for you, knowing you are always reaching for them. In the name of Christ we pray. Amen.

Part IV

**Wedding Resources
for the Pastor**

Wedding Resources for the Pastor

Pastor as a Resource

For most people, planning and celebrating a wedding is a completely new experience. Most everyone has attended a wedding or two; some have participated as bridesmaids or groomsmen. Parents remember their own and have a vague recollection of procedure, protocol, expectations, and practices, but so much of that has faded into a distant memory. There are a limited number of books on weddings and a limited number of people, save florists and wedding consultants in larger communities, who have a great amount of knowledge about how to carry out a wedding from beginning to end. Where does a couple turn and how do they know how to plan and what resources are available?

The pastor is often the first line of defense, or offense, whichever the case may be, and a pastor who has equipped himself/herself properly will be a great resource for the couple, church, and community. The pastor should have a working knowledge of weddings, protocol, and procedure, as well as be a contact and referral person for needs as they may arise.

Wedding Guidelines

Each pastor and each church should have their own set guidelines for performing weddings. A set of guidelines should be developed if such does not exist. Guidelines are important for the church, the pastor, and the couple as they set parameters of expectations for everyone involved. Having written guidelines available enables the couple to review them and have a working knowledge of what a particular pastor or church will allow or not allow. Most often grooms and brides come from different church traditions and do not know what to expect from the other's religious body. Guidelines are thus very helpful for everyone, as they clearly spell out expectations.

Pre-written guidelines protect the pastor from being pressured into putting something into the service with which the pastor is uncomfortable. With much media focus on weddings today and much information available from the internet, couples may bring requests that are outside the parameters or rubric of a given pastor or church's acceptable standards or ritual. It is easier to be proactive by presenting pre-written guidelines up front, than to be caught in a trap by some eccentric request to include something that would be unacceptable. Guidelines avoid these misunderstandings and relieve the pastor from being caught in the middle. Simply put, guidelines are policy, and the authority of policy is with the church and not the pastor.

The pastor may choose to have some flexibility with guidelines. That is understandable in certain circumstances. No pastor wants to come across as rigid and inflexible. It is, however, much easier to allow a special request under the guidance of guidelines, than simply to be "shooting from the hip" regarding special requests.

Guidelines are most helpful to the prospective bride and groom. By having written guidelines in hand, the couple and their families are able to move forward with the assurance that they are doing everything properly and in accordance with the established rules of the church. The pastor will find that guidelines are welcomed as positive tools as they simply do what the root of the word implies, that is to guide.

Guidelines may also protect the couple from undue pressures from florists, photographers, and wedding consultants to sell their wares. While these adjunct people may be important to the wedding service, they are in the business to sell and may overkill the service marketing their products. After all, who wants a videographer running down the aisle after the bride or who comes to a wedding for a floral show? Established guidelines place the burden of what is acceptable and proper on the policy or institution and not on the couple, relieving them from the stress of having either to say "no" or to tone down the proposals of those who are marketing their products and services.

For all of the above reasons, it is strongly suggested that any church that does not have an established set of guidelines develop one. Guidelines reflecting the particular policies, resources, and settings of the local church should be carefully developed and approved by the governance board. The following samples of guidelines may be helpful in developing new guidelines or augmenting existing ones.

First Church

Street Address or Post Office Box
City, State, Zip Code

Wedding Guidelines

A wedding is one of the happiest and holiest moments in life. As two people join their lives to establish a Christian home, the church rejoices with them and is eager to help make the occasion beautiful and meaningful. A wedding does not have to be elaborate in order to be beautiful. The true beauty lies in the spirit and attitude of those who take part, their sincerity, and a deep sense of the presence of God.

We are happy you are having your wedding at First Church and have developed these guidelines to assist you as you make your plans for your wedding.

Planning Your Wedding

Arrangements

Couples should chose the date and time for their wedding and rehearsal as early as possible and confirm the chosen date with the church office. A reservation fee of $100.00 is required in order to reserve the sanctuary or chapel. On receiving the reservation fee, the church office schedules the couple an appointment with the pastor who will be officiating at the service. The pastor meets with the couple and sets up a schedule of appointments for premarital counseling and planning for the wedding. Both the prospective bride and groom should be present for this initial meeting.

It is the policy of First Church that one of our ministers conduct all marriage ceremonies in this church. Outside clergy and friends may participate only to the extent of giving a prayer or reading or in some limited fashion. The sanctuary of First Church seats 500 people. The chapel seats 80.

Weddings may be scheduled on most days with the exception of religious and secular holidays including Christmas, New Year's, Memorial Day, Independence Day, Labor Day, and Thanksgiving. Because of the highly religious importance of Holy Week and the time constraints of the pastors, weddings are not scheduled during this time.

Music

The church considers the wedding ceremony to be a sacred service. Therefore only music suitable for a worship service at First Church may be considered. The Director of Music is in charge of all music at the church including weddings and will gladly assist couples in planning appropriate music for their service. The church organist plays for all weddings unless he/she grants permission for an outside organist to play, and in this case the Director of Music or organist must approve all musical selections even though he/she is not playing.

It is not necessary to have vocalists or instrumentalists as a part of the service unless the couple wishes to do so. However, if vocalists or instrumentalists are included, they should be selected with care. Only well-trained musicians should be invited, as music is an integral part of the wedding. The Director of Music will assist couples in locating and selecting musicians in the event the couple needs assistance. It is not necessary for these special musicians to attend the rehearsal, but they should meet with the Director of Music/organist to review the music prior to the wedding.

The Rehearsal

Allow an hour for rehearsal. Be punctual. Rehearsals should begin promptly.

The officiating pastor and wedding coordinator will be present at the rehearsal. The coordinator will walk through the mechanics of the service twice including the seating of parents and special guests. The pastor will review the service in its entirety once and the rubrics of the service a second time as needed.

All members of the bridal party should attend, including parents of the bride and groom.

Flowers and Church Decorations

Both the sanctuary and the chapel of First Church are places of exquisite and dignified beauty. Neither requires extensive decorations in order to make them attractive for wedding services. The following suggestions are given to preserve the spiritual atmosphere in the church and safeguard the furnishings.

Only the following items are to be placed on the altar: the two existing candles, the large Bible, the unity candle holder and either two flower arrangements in the existing vases or a single arrangement placed between the candles. Liners for the vases may be obtained from the church office.

The only appropriate altar floral arrangements are created with fresh cut flowers and/or greenery.

Two brass candelabras are available for use at no charge. An aisle runner is not necessary, but may be ordered through your florist if you desire. The church will supply candles for the candelabras as well as the unity candle, except for the large center candle. Unity candles may be ordered through the church office or obtained locally at a Christian book store or bridal shop.

The furniture and floor must be fully protected at all times from moisture and candle wax. Staples, nails, tape, and other items that may cause damage must not be used on the pews or elsewhere. Persons responsible for decorating will also be responsible for any damage done to the building or furniture. Included with these guidelines is a document that may be given to the florist setting forth the requirements of the church with regards to decorations. The florist should check with the pastor or church administrator regarding placement of decorations at times when there will be access to the church.

All decorations should be removed immediately after the wedding so that the sanctuary or chapel is ready for other church functions. Flowers left on the altar will be used for church services and/or given to area home-bounds or hospital patients.

Photography and Videography
Photographs and videos are good ways to remember your special day. Professional photographers and videographers should be chosen with care in order to ensure the quality of good pictures. In order to preserve the dignity of the service, the following guidelines have been established for photographs and videos:

No photographs are to be taken in the sanctuary after guests begin to arrive or at any time during the service with the following exceptions:

• One time exposure may be taken from the rear of the sanctuary if the photographer uses a camera that is silent.

• One photograph may be taken as the bride enters the last couple of pews and one may be taken as the bride and groom approach the rear of the sanctuary.

When the service is completed, the wedding party may return to the sanctuary for the taking of pictures.

Video equipment must be stationary at the designated place for the entire service and must be set up prior to the arrival of guests.

Dressing for the Wedding
The church has provided special areas for dressing for the bride and her attendants as well as the groom and his groomsmen.

The bride and her attendants may dress in the women's parlor near the foyer of the church. Bathroom facilities and mirrors are amply available. It is, however, recommended that as much preparation as possible (hair, nails, makeup, etc.) be done prior to arriving at the church. Dresses and shoes may be brought to the church the day prior to the wedding or at the time of rehearsal, but the bridal party should check with the church office.

The groom and groomsmen may also change at the church. The conference room located behind the sanctuary is the groom's designated place for dressing. It is recommended that one groomsman be responsible for gathering and counting all articles (cummerbunds, studs, cuff links, etc.) included in the formal wear.

It is expected that the bridal party remove all articles of apparel, boxes, and other items immediately following the wedding.

Responsibility for the Safekeeping of Personal Items

The church will make every effort to protect personal items brought to the church for the wedding. The building generally remains locked when the office is closed. However, the church cannot be held liable if personal items are lost, stolen, or damaged. It is recommended that purses, money, or jewelry not be left unattended.

Miscellaneous Information

Church membership at First Church is not a requirement in order to be married in the church. However, non-members are expected to abide by the same guidelines as members.

If the couple would like to leave the altar flowers for the following Sunday morning services, this request should be made with the church office as early as possible.

The throwing of rice or birdseed is not allowed inside or outside the church following the wedding. Balloons or bubbles may be used outside the church.

Premarital counseling is required by the pastors for all couples married in the church. Each pastor has his/her own set of counseling requirements and will review those at the initial meeting. The counseling requirement is to ensure satisfactory guidance so that your marriage begins on a solid foundation and that the service has meaning and dignity.

While membership at First Church is not a requirement, the pastors encourage every couple to make their marriage a Christian one and to find a place of worship mutually meaningful to both the wife and husband. First Church welcomes you to begin your marriage as members of this church where you will find a circle of friends and support for the launching of your marriage. You may speak with one of the pastors if you desire to unite with the membership of this church.

Please remember that it is your responsibility to make the arrangements to meet with the officiating pastor and music director. You should call the church office to set up these appointments soon after your wedding date has been placed on the church calendar.

First Church has a Wedding Guild of trained wedding coordinators who are available to help you with your wedding. The assigned coordinator will be available to assist you with any questions you may have regarding your wedding. She will attend and oversee the rehearsal and will be present to orchestrate the mechanics of the wedding itself. The coordinator is to see that everything runs smoothly during the rehearsal and at the wedding itself.

Information

for your

Florist

and

Photographer

First Church

City, State

Information for the Florist

We are pleased that you have been asked to participate in a wedding at First Church. We look forward to working with you and hope the following guidelines will be of help to you as you plan the floral arrangements and decorations for the upcoming wedding.

Our sanctuary is a place of exquisite and dignified beauty. It does not require extensive decoration to make it a place for beautiful services such as weddings. The following guidelines are given to preserve the spiritual atmosphere and safeguard the furnishings of the church.

No decorations are to be placed on the altar other than the regular appointments: the two existing candles, the large Bible, the unity candle holder, and either two flower arrangements in the existing vases or a single arrangement placed between the two candles. Liners for the vases may be obtained through the church office.

The only appropriate flower arrangements for the sanctuary or chapel are fresh cut flowers or greenery.

The church provides two brass candelabras and candles to couples at no charge. The chancel does not lend itself to an over abundance of additional greenery. The florist should check with the church administrator or officiating pastor on the placement of additional decorations. An aisle runner is not necessary, but is permissible if the couple so desires.

The church furniture, carpet, and flooring must be protected at all times. Staples, nails, tape, and other items that may cause damage must not be used on the pews or elsewhere. Persons responsible for decorating the church will be responsible for any damage done to the building or furniture.

The florist may supply pew markers (greenery with bows) for reserved seating if the couple so desires. These markers may be attached to the pews in a way that causes no damage to the pews.

All decorations should be removed immediately following the wedding in order for the church to be ready for other services.

First Church

City, State

Information for the Photographer

First Church is happy that you will be participating in an upcoming wedding and wants to help you and the wedding party in every way possible with your task of recording this special time in the lives of this couple with photographs or videos. The staff of First Church strives to see that all weddings go as smoothly as possible for all concerned. The church has established certain policies and guidelines to assist you with regards to photography and videography. We trust these guidelines will assist you as you, together with us, strive to do the very best job for the wedding couple.

No photographs are to be taken in the sanctuary or chapel after guests begin to arrive, or at any time during the service with the following exceptions:

• One time exposure may be made from the rear of the sanctuary if the photographer uses a camera that is silent.

• One photograph may be taken as the bride enters the last couple of pews and one may be taken as the bride and groom approach the rear of the sanctuary.

When the service is completed, the wedding party may return to the sanctuary for the taking of wedding pictures.

Video equipment must be stationary at the designated place for the entire service and must be set up prior to the wedding. The pastor or wedding coordinator will be available for instruction on designated stations for video equipment.

First Church

City, State

Wedding Information Sheet

Wedding Date _____ Time _____

Rehearsal Date _____ Time _____

* * * * * * *

Bride's Name _____ Age _____

Home Address _____

Home Phone _____ Business Phone _____

Parents' Names and Address(es) if applicable _____

_____

Church or Religious Affiliation _____

* * * * * * *

Groom's Name _____ Age _____

Home Address _____

Home Phone _____ Business Phone _____

Parents' Names and Address(es) if applicable _____

_____

* * * * * * *

Number of guests expected _____

Is this a second marriage for either? _____ Children? _____

Maid or Matron of Honor _____ Best Man _____

Bridesmaids _____

_____

_____

Groomsmen _____

_____

_____

Will you be using?

Flower girl _____ Unity Candle _____ Candelabras _____ Aisle Runner _____

Ring Bearer _____ Single or Double Ring Ceremony _____ Kneeling Bench _____

Special Readings _____

Special Music Requested _____

Church Organist _____ Vocalists _____

Instrumentalists _____

_____

Please supply us with the names and phone numbers for your:

Florist _____ Phone number _____

Photographer _____ Phone number _____

Videographer _____ Phone number _____

Rehearsal Dinner, Time and Place _____

Reception, Time and Place _____

Couple's Anticipated Permanent Address _____

Christ Church

**Street Address or Post Office Box
City, State, Zip Code**

Wedding Guidelines

A Message to the Bride and Groom

Date

Dear Friends:

Weddings are times of joy and covenant ... and yes, confusion. The joy and the covenant are wonderful and Christ Church looks forward to sharing these with you. We even look forward to ironing out the confusion! As you begin your journey together, you are joining a long line of couples who have affirmed and shared their commitment to a Christian marriage and to each other since this church's founding more than 100 years ago.

A wedding in this church is first and foremost a service of worship celebrating the presence and the blessing of God.

This booklet should help you with many of the questions couples often ask. Please take the time to read the material we provide. It's important and we will assume you understand and agree to live with it. You will also have your own questions and we look forward to helping you find answers.

Congratulations on your wedding!

Sincerely,

Christ Church

Wedding Arrangements

Arrangements for weddings are made through the church office and the wedding coordinator. All couples wishing to be married at Christ Church must present a marriage license to the officiating pastor at the time of the rehearsal. A pastor of this church must officiate at all weddings taking place in the sanctuary or on the grounds of this church. Other ordained clergy may be invited to participate, but such participation should be discussed with the officiating pastor before setting such arrangements in motion. Pastors of this church shall normally be the "minister of record" for marriages witnessed in this church. The governing board of the church supports any pastor's right to decline to perform a ceremony.

All plans must be discussed with the wedding coordinator and the officiating pastor before any wedding arrangements are completed. Christ Church is committed to accommodating those who sincerely wish to be married in this church. If either the bride or groom is a member of Christ Church, then the couple may express a preference for a particular pastor. If neither the bride nor groom is a member of the church, then the pastoral leadership for the service is at the discretion of the church staff. The officiating pastor will be responsible for and have authority over both the arrangements and the service. **No date is confirmed until after the couple has met with the officiating minister for the initial counseling interview.**

A Wedding Information and Wedding Contract form must be completed and submitted to the wedding coordinator by the couple. This application must be approved by one of the pastors in order that the appropriate facilities may be reserved and the proper people involved be notified. A non-refundable deposit fee is required at the time of the application to reserve the time and date of the wedding. The total fee must be paid one month prior to the wedding.

Multiple weddings may occur at Christ Church during any given week. It is therefore advisable to schedule rehearsal times two or three days prior to the wedding. Scheduling this time must be done through the wedding coordinator.

Premarital consultation with a Christ Church pastor is a pre-requisite for any wedding held at Christ Church.

The Sanctuary

The sanctuary of Christ Church is dedicated to the worship of God. Any service that takes place in the church must therefore be in keeping with the high purpose to which the church has been dedicated.

The rehearsal and the wedding will be conducted with dignity and in a Christian spirit. Members of the wedding party and guests must conduct themselves in an acceptable manner of behavior while in the sanctuary or on the grounds of the church. Alcoholic beverages or smoking are not allowed on the premises. No food is allowed in the sanctuary. The bride and groom and their parents are responsible for the conduct of the wedding guests.

Christian Symbols

The pulpit, the lectern, the baptismal font, and the cross and candles on the altar are Christian symbols that have significant meaning and must not be moved or hidden from view under any circumstances for any wedding.

Special Important Regulations

No flower petals, rice, or birdseed may be dropped in the church or on the church grounds. The releasing of doves is not permitted.

Real wedding rings are to be in the care of adults and are not to be placed on the ring pillow.

Children under the age of three are not allowed to be a part of the wedding party.

Wedding and Rehearsal Time

Because of the number of weddings and other church events scheduled at Christ Church, it is imperative that both rehearsals and weddings begin on time. It is not possible to wait for latecomers as such may run the service into the next scheduled event.

Flowers

Florists should check with the wedding coordinator regarding the arrangement of flowers. The rule of thumb with flowers is that excessive flower arrangements detract from the wedding and the beauty of the chancel. No arrangement may hide the important symbols of the church, including the cross, the candles, the Bible, the pulpit, and the lectern. Aisle cloths are not allowed as the aisle is fully carpeted. Pew markers may be affixed with pipe cleaners, rubber bands, or satin ribbons. Scotch tape is not allowed. Nothing may be attached by screws, tacks, or clamps. Bridal couples must make their florist aware of the following rules:

No tape of any kind, thumbtacks, nails, screws, or clamps may be used on the church pews or furniture.

The liturgical cloths on the altar, pulpit, and lectern are not to be moved.

Only candles supplied by the church may be used, the exception being the unity candle.

Aisle runners may not be used.

Flowers must be placed so that the cross, candles, Bible, pulpit, or lectern are not obstructed from view.

The church is available for decorations two hours prior to the wedding.

All decorations must be removed immediately following the wedding.

Music

Prelude Music

The prelude sets the tone for the wedding. The organist generally begins playing a selection of classical music fifteen minutes prior to the bridal processional. Couples who have special requests for music should inform the organist four weeks prior to the wedding. While the church seeks to accommodate reasonable requests, some may be denied because either the piece does not play well on the organ or because it is deemed as not appropriate for a church wedding.

Some couples prefer instrumental music for the prelude. Several choices are available including: the harp, violin, or string ensemble/woodwind ensemble. The music staff is able to put couples in contact with these musicians.

Vocal Soloists

Many couples like to have vocal soloists perform at their wedding. The music staff of Christ Church offers a wide repertory of music and will sing most requests within the following guidelines:

All secular songs (popular music) must be sung before the ceremony begins.

All selections must sound well when accompanied by the organ or piano.

All selections must be given to the soloist(s) at least four weeks prior to the wedding.

All selections must be determined by the church staff to be appropriate for use in a church wedding.

The Christ Church staff reserves the right to refuse any selection believed to be contrary to any of these guidelines.

Musicians Outside the Church Staff

Couples may occasionally request a soloist or instrumentalist of their own choosing, be that a friend or relative. Generally these requests can be accommodated with the exception of the organist. Any couple who wishes to have someone outside the church staff perform should follow these guidelines:

The soloist must have experience singing in public.

The soloist must contact the organist at least four weeks in advance of the wedding.

The soloist is responsible for bringing copies of the selected music to the organist.

The soloist will rehearse with the organist either at the rehearsal or no less than one hour before the service.

All musical arrangements must be finalized in writing and submitted to the Wedding Coordinator two weeks prior to the wedding.

Pictures

Christ Church is a house of worship and therefore requests that all photography and videography be unobtrusive. Videotaping is to be done with the permission of the wedding director and only by using existing light. The videographer must stay in one place in the choir loft. Both the photographer and the videographer must check with the wedding director before setting up. Obtrusive equipment or activity detracts from the dignity and the beauty of the service.

Photos

Because of scheduling limitations, the start of the wedding must not be delayed by picture taking. If pictures of the bride are to be made upon her arrival, she should arrive early to accommodate the needed space of time.

The photographer should be careful not to interfere with members of the wedding party. He/she should keep a low profile as the focus of the wedding is on the service which should not be detracted from by the taking of pictures.

Photographs are not allowed during the service except for time-released photos.

The wedding party and photographer must be out of the sanctuary no later than one hour after the scheduled time for the wedding.

Videos

Videographers must work with existing light. No external light sources will be allowed.

Video cameras must work with battery packs as electrical outlets are not available for use.

The videographer must remain stationary in the choir loft during the service. He/she is not allowed to move around during the service.

Bride's Room

The church provides the bride and her attendants a dressing room if they wish to dress at the church. The room is available one hour before and one hour after the service. Please do not leave purses or valuables in the room during the wedding. Drinking and smoking are not allowed in the bride's or groom's room. Furniture should not be moved and all personal belongings should be removed upon leaving the room.

Sample III

The Community Church

Street Address
City, State

Getting Married at Community Church
Guidelines for Celebrating Your Special Day

A Message from the Pastor

Other than when one comes to faith in Jesus Christ, there is no time in life that is quite so momentous, as beautiful, or so hopeful as a wedding. Laughter rings through the hectic hours of preparation. The prayers of family and the hopes of a lifetime converge in a single event. God intends that the wedding and marriage be a celebration of love and loyalty.

God designed Christian marriage for his people. Therefore, the wedding is a worship service and a time to honor the One who is as present at your wedding as he was at the wedding in Cana of Galilee.

We at Community Church are biblically based and Christ-honoring. We believe, as did our Lord, that this is a lifelong covenant commitment launched by heartfelt vows and the pledging of undying love. May God richly bless you as you pray and plan. May you not only fall in love, but grow in love.

Grace and peace,

The Senior Pastor

Officiating Pastor

Normally, one of the pastors of Community Church officiates at weddings held at the church. In the event the couple wishes to be married by a pastor not related to Community Church, the Senior Pastor of Community must be consulted. Subsequent to approval, and according to ministerial ethics, the Senior Pastor will write a letter to the pastor, inviting him/her to officiate.

It is policy of each staff pastor to counsel with the bride and groom at least one month prior to the wedding, so that the true meaning of a Christian marriage may be understood. Appointments may be made by calling the pastor's secretary. It is the pastor's sincere desire that this be one of the most significant moments of your life

Scheduling a Wedding

A couple planning a wedding at Community Church will need a minimum of 3-4 months for planning, scheduling, and preparation. This is necessary due to the amount of time required for pre-marital counseling and the church calendaring process. The earlier a couple begins the process, the more likely they will get their preferred date and time. Couples may schedule a wedding at Community in the following manner:

Contact the ministry assistant in the Pastoral Care Office. The ministry assistant will "temporarily" schedule your wedding date and mail a copy of the Community Marriage Covenant and Church Wedding Brochure to you.

Within two weeks of receiving the information, the couple should schedule the initial pre-marital counseling appointment with the officiating pastor. If the couple is unsure which pastor is available, the ministry assistant in the Pastoral Care Office is available to assist.

During the initial pre-marital counseling appointment, the officiating pastor will give approval for the wedding to take place at Community and assign a mentoring couple to counsel the engaged couple.

The couple is encouraged to attend one of the marriage enrichment classes held at Community. These classes are made up of both married and engaged couples who meet on a regular basis for both fellowship and the enhancement of their relationships. It is recommended that couples continue to be a part of the marriage enrichment classes after their marriage at either Community or the faith family the couple is a part of. Marriage enrichment places couples in a positive environment with other couples who believe in the sanctity and well-being of marriage.

The date requested is "temporarily" placed on the main church calendar, but is not actually considered calendared in until the pastor performing the ceremony has given his approval. Once a couple has received this approval, they may contact the Wedding Director to begin discussing all the needed details relating to the wedding.

Wedding Director

Our church Wedding Director is responsible for scheduling times of decorating, rehearsal, and the actual wedding on the church calendar. All weddings are ultimately scheduled through the director. Weddings may not be scheduled on Sundays or holidays. Dates are calendared in after couples have received approval by the officiating pastor.

The Wedding Director will mail couples a wedding booking sheet which is to be completed and returned to her. The couple will need to make an appointment with her at least six weeks prior to the wedding to go over all the details of the wedding.

The Wedding Director will direct the rehearsal and will be present at least an hour and a half before the ceremony to coordinate all the preparations and direct the wedding. She will help plan and supervise the reception if the reception is to be held on church property.

Flowers

In the placing of flowers, palms, or other decorations, care must be taken to ensure that the floors, carpets, walls, and furnishings not be damaged. Decorations must not be hung or suspended from fixtures or furnishings. Except for family pew markers, no decorations may be attached to the furniture. Nails, tacks, or screws of any type are not allowed. Masking tape may be used, but Scotch tape is not allowed.

The florist engaged by the bride and groom shall be responsible for all decorating and must remove all decorations immediately following the wedding. A member of the custodial staff must be present while the florist decorates or removes the decorations.

Music

It is our desire that the music selected would honor our Lord and be in keeping with the dignity of a service of worship.

Examples of appropriate vocal texts would be categorized as worship or testimony. Songs that invite the Lord into your home and marriage are encouraged. Acceptable instrumental music may be drawn from the above categories, from classics that are time honored, or from various musical style periods.

Secular love songs are considered inappropriate for the wedding service, but may be used at the reception. Music to be used must be cleared in advance with the Minister of Music who will also be happy to assist couples with their music selections.

Music should be given to the musicians at least two weeks before the wedding date for their preparation.

Arrangements for vocalists and instrumentalists should be handled privately, although the Minister of Music will be happy to suggest the names of qualified and experienced singers and instrumentalists. It is the responsibility of the bride to see that the vocalists contact the accompanists or sound technicians to arrange a rehearsal. This rehearsal should be at a time other than the wedding rehearsal.

Photographs

Pictures are a cherished part of weddings. Because a wedding is a sacred occasion, Community Church requests that these procedures be followed in the taking of photographs.

Flash pictures may be taken during the processional and recessional. No flash photography is allowed during the ceremony. The wedding party will reassemble to recreate scenes from the wedding following the ceremony according to the wishes of the couple.

There is no restriction on taking pictures during the reception.

The Wedding Party

It is expected that members of the wedding party will recognize the fact that this is a church and will conduct themselves in a manner befitting the atmosphere of a place of worship at all times.

Immediately prior to both the rehearsal and wedding, it is expected that members of the wedding party refrain from the use of alcoholic beverages.

Smoking is not permitted anywhere in the church building or grounds. It is the obligation of the bride and groom to make certain that these policies are made known to and followed by all members of the wedding party.

Rooms are available for the bride and her attendants and the groom and his groomsmen to dress at the church. Arrangements for these rooms may be made through the Wedding Director. Since the church cannot be responsible for personal belongings, the church requests that personal items be removed from these rooms before the wedding.

Receptions

All receptions for the church will be held either in the Life Enrichment Center or in the Fellowship Hall. Arrangements for these facilities must be made through the Wedding Director.

The church has tables, chairs, refrigeration, and a catering kitchen for use during the reception. The church has a No Smoking and No Alcohol policy. There will be no exceptions to this policy.

Initial Introduction Letter

Dear (names),

We are happy to make notation of your wedding scheduled for (date) at _____ p.m.

I am enclosing our wedding brochure which contains information pertaining to policies and procedures governing all weddings at Community Church.

If you have not made an appointment for you and your fiancé for pre-marital counseling, you will need to do that right away. You may do this by calling the church office and scheduling the appointment. It is the wish of your officiating pastor that your wedding be one of the most significant moments of your life; therefore do not hesitate to ask any questions of him/her.

You will need to make an appointment with me approximately one month prior to the date of your wedding to finalize the details of your rehearsal and wedding. I have enclosed a wedding booking sheet to assist me in directing your wedding. Please fill this out and bring it with you for our appointment.

I have enclosed a letter for you to give to the florist and one for the photographer explaining church policy regarding decorations and photography at Community Church.

You should also call the church office as soon as possible to make an appointment with the Minister of Music. He will be most happy to counsel with you concerning the musical arrangements for your wedding.

If you have any questions, please do not hesitate to call. I will be most happy to assist you.

Sincerely,

Church Wedding Director

TO: THE PHOTOGRAPHER

BRIDE:

DATE AND HOUR OF WEDDING:

This letter is to inform you of church policy regarding the taking of wedding pictures. Because a wedding is a sacred occasion, these procedures must be followed.

Flash cameras may not be used during the ceremony. For the recessional, the photographer must stand at the end of the aisle to take pictures. He/she is not allowed to walk down the center aisle, as this is obtrusive.

The wedding party will return to the sanctuary to pose for pictures immediately following the ceremony. They will be instructed at the rehearsal to cooperate with the photographer so that he/she will be able to take pictures as quickly as possible in order that the reception may not be unduly delayed.

There is no restriction on taking pictures during the reception.

Sincerely,

Wedding Director

TO: FLORIST

BRIDE:

DATE AND HOUR OF WEDDING:

This letter is to inform you of church policy regarding decorations for a wedding at Community Church.

Any candles used must be chase, paradise, or metal candles. We have found that even dripless candles do drip because of the movement of air from vents. A large piece of plastic or visqueen must be placed under each candelabra.

In the placing of flowers, palms, or other decorations, care must be taken to ensure that floors, carpets, walls, or furnishings are not damaged.

Decorations must not be hung or suspended from fixtures or furnishings. Except for the family pew, no decorations may be attached to furniture. Nails, screws, or Scotch tape are not allowed.

The church will need to be notified as to the time the church needs to be open for decorating and deliveries. I, as Wedding Director, am at the church one hour before the wedding.

All decorations must be removed from the sanctuary as soon as possible following the wedding. The florist is responsible for any damage due to decorations used.

All bridal and attendants' bouquets, corsages, and boutonnieres must be delivered to the church at least one hour prior to the wedding. It is very helpful to tag the flowers as to whom they go.

Thank you for your cooperation.

Sincerely,

Wedding Director

Wedding Fee Samples

Sample I

Schedule of Wedding Fees

There are no fees for use of the sanctuary for members of Christ Church. The bride or groom or their immediate families must currently be members of the church.

Anyone using the sanctuary, including church members for whom there is no sanctuary fee, is required to make an advance deposit of $100 in order to reserve the sanctuary. This deposit is refundable to members, provided there is no damage to church property and provided there are no serious violations of this wedding policy, such as the presence of alcohol or drugs or the throwing of rice. In the event of damage in excess of the deposit, there will be an additional billing to cover the damage and expense to the church.

Fees

	MEMBERS	NON-MEMBERS
Fees for use of the Sanctuary	$ 0	$250
Fees for use of the Chapel	$ 0	$150
Officiating Pastor (*For members, the Pastor's honorarium is suggested at the discretion of the bride and groom. The fee for non-members includes premarital counseling, rehearsal, and the wedding ceremony.)	Honorarium	$200*
The Organist/Director of Music (Includes consultation, rehearsal, and wedding. There is a $50 rehearsal fee if using a soloist or instrumentalist.)	$125	$175
The Wedding Director	$100	$100
The Custodian	$ 75	$ 75

Separate payment envelopes provided by the Wedding Director should be sent to the church office at least one week prior to the wedding.

Sample II

Wedding Expenses

There is no charge to church members for use of the Sanctuary or Fellowship Hall.

The charge to **non-members** ** is as follows:

Wedding in the Sanctuary	$525
Use of the Fellowship Hall	$150
Use of the Welcome Center	$75
Wedding Director	$150

The charge for non-members having a wedding in the sanctuary includes the use of the facility and operating expenses, custodial services for the rehearsal and the wedding, and an honorarium for the officiating pastor. Arrangements for the organist and vocalists are made separately.

The charge for **members** is as follows:

Wedding in the Sanctuary	$175
Reception	$100
Welcome Center	$50
Wedding Director	$100
Officiating Pastor	Love Gift

The charge for a wedding in the sanctuary includes the use of the facility and custodial services for the rehearsal and the wedding.

The Love Gift for the officiating pastor is traditionally the responsibility of the groom and is given on the wedding day.

Arrangements for the organist and soloist are made separately. Please contact the organist directly by calling the church office.

Payments are expected prior to the wedding date.

Non-members are to write one check for the total amount. Please make the payment out to The Community Church.

Sample III

Wedding Fees

DEPOSIT

A deposit of $100 is required to reserve the church for a wedding. The deposit will be forfeited in the event of a wedding cancellation. The deposit will be refunded the week following the ceremony if the wedding has stayed within the time limits and if there has been no damage to church property.

WEDDING FEES

Deposit	$100
Sanctuary Wedding	$300
Chapel Wedding	$150
Minister	$175
Organist*	$125
Soloist	$75
Candelabras	$50
Unity Candle Base	$25
Audio or Video Recordings	$35
The church will print bulletins provided by the wedding party with one week's lead time.	$50
*There is an additional charge for the organist to rehearse with the soloist.	$25

All fees are to be paid 10 days prior to the rehearsal. The fees are based on the assumption that the rehearsal will last no longer than one hour and the wedding and picture-taking will last no longer than one to one and a half hours. An additional custodial fee will be assessed if these limits are exceeded. The bridal couple is financially accountable for any damage to the church.

Wedding Guild/Directors

Whether churches do a large or small number of weddings, it is a good idea to have a trained group of wedding coordinators to assist the pastor and the wedding couple with wedding plans as they involve the church. A Wedding Guild made up of a cadre of trained directors will prove to be an invaluable asset. Churches that do an exceptionally large amount of weddings may have a wedding coordinator as a part of their staff.

Training for members of the Wedding Guild may come from the wedding coordinator, a resource person in the community, or the pastor him/herself. Protocol for weddings may be obtained from any bookstore or even off the internet. To facilitate such a guild, the pastor and/or the wedding coordinator needs to advertise a training event several weeks in advance as well as seek out recruits who may have a special gift for this ministry.

Printed Procedures and Wedding Etiquette

As resource material for the Wedding Guild and Wedding Coordinator, having printed material available for training and review is a necessity. Guild members tend to forget the protocol if there is much time between the times when they are called upon to do weddings. The handout is not only a refresher for them, but serves as a guide for the wedding party should questions arise.

Wedding Director/Wedding Guild Member

Below are some basic guidelines for Wedding Directors/Wedding Guild Members. The director should:

- Make contact with the bridal couple as soon as the wedding is confirmed and on the church calendar. Reassure them that you will be there to assist in any way possible to make their wedding a beautiful, spiritual, and memorable one.

- Meet with the couple to review the service and rehearsal.

- Be at the rehearsal in ample time to greet the wedding party as they arrive for rehearsal.

- Be at the church two hours before the wedding to ensure that everything is ready for the arrival of the wedding party, florist, photographer, and others needful for the wedding.

- Remain at the wedding site to ensure that everything is in order for the service that is to follow.

The Rehearsal

The rehearsal is an opportunity to review the ceremony in preparation for the actual service. In this sense, it is a "pre-service." Here the bride and groom have the occasion to experience the wedding in a more relaxed atmosphere, in addition to making any last minute requests to the wedding director.

The pastor, director, and music director should review the service so that everyone involved will feel comfortable as to what to expect. The rehearsal should begin with an invocation as the rehearsal is also a service within itself.

After the minister has given a welcome and offered a prayer, the wedding director should also welcome everyone and introduce the bride and groom, the immediate wedding party, and the parents of the couple. It is important for the director or wedding guild member to **take charge**, as wedding rehearsals usually flounder without someone commanding the leadership. By now the director should be well acquainted with the wishes of the bride and groom. The director should have a demeanor of expertise regarding what should happen at the rehearsal and wedding. While there is no need to be controlling, lack of a "take charge" attitude will only create anxiety on the part of the bride and groom that they are not "in good hands." The director should not be constantly asking guidance from the bride. The bride is expecting the director to be the one who knows what is proper and constant questioning of the bride only creates apprehension. It is best for the director to come across as "the expert" on weddings. Following are procedures for the director to follow at the rehearsal.

After introductions, the director should position each member of the wedding party in his/her position as they will be in the wedding. When everyone is in place, the director should allow the pastor the opportunity to go through the service verbally as well as assist him/her with the mechanics of the service as needed. The director may walk the wedding party through the mechanics of the service again as need be.

After practicing the mechanics of the service, the director should gather the wedding party together to review what is expected at the wedding with regards to:

- Where the wedding party will dress.

- What time members of the wedding party should arrive.

- What the responsibilities of each member of the wedding party are.

- Transportation to the church.

- Transportation to the reception.

- Any special needs of the wedding party.

When the director is satisfied that everyone understands both the service and other pertinent concerns, she/he then has a time of special training for parents, groomsmen, and other people who have particular functions in the service.

Review for the Groomsmen would be as follows:

- Groomsmen should seat all guests.

- Ushering should be done with dignity and precision. Walking upright looks far better than slumping over. Even giving ushering a sense of military crispness offers an effect of decorum and formality.

- Groomsmen should ask the guests whether they would like to sit on the bride's or groom's side of the sanctuary, but should also keep some balance if it appears seating is out of balance. The groom's side is the right side facing the front and the bride's is the left.

- The groomsmen should escort all female guests by extending their right arm and escorting them down the aisle, followed by the male in the party. Once the usher-groomsman has reached the desired seat, he should hold the female guest to one side and invite the male guest to be seated first. This allows the female to have the more desired inside seating. If there is more than one female, each should be escorted. Female guests should never be escorted in a group. Such sends the wrong message of their importance and proper place as wedding guests.

- Male guests who are not accompanied by females, should be walked down the aisle and shown a seat. Males should not be left to find their own seats.

- When escorting someone to their seat, the usher-groomsman should stop at the pew, turn toward the vacant seat and indicate this is the seat of the guests. The groomsman should wait until the guest is seated before turning to walk away. If other guests are already seated, the usher-groomsman should request that they move down the pew in order to make room for the newly arrived guest.

Honored Guests

Honored guests include parents, grandparents, and special relatives or friends whom the couple wishes to honor with special seating. Reserved markers (ribbons, flowers, or pew markers) indicate the pews are reserved for honored guests. Normally, special guests sit in the third row from the front, grandparents in the second row, and parents sit in the first row.

Ushers should seat the special guests in reverse order in terms of their relationship to the bridal couple; that is, special friends or special relatives who occupy the third or fourth row of special seating should be seated first, grandparents second, and parents last. Ushers should seat the special guests in an alternating manner so that the groom's special guests are seated first, the bride's special guests seated second, the groom's grandparents seated third, the bride's grandparents seated fourth, the groom's parents seated fifth, and the mother of the bride, who has the place of honor, seated last.

Following the recessional, the ushers-groomsmen will escort the special guests out in reverse order from which they were seated, that is the bride's mother and her husband are the first to be escorted out, followed by the groom's parents, followed by the bride's grandparents, followed by the groom's grandparents, etc. The rule of thumb is: Last in — First out/First in — Last out. The wedding coordinator must be at the rear of the sanctuary to prompt the ushers immediately after the wedding party has exited the sanctuary. Many groomsmen will forget they are to return to usher out the special guests, thus it is incumbent on the wedding director to see that this is done.

The rehearsal should begin promptly. Rehearsals should never take over an hour and the director should move the rehearsal along in a timely fashion. Promptness is particularly important in view of the fact that a rehearsal dinner follows. The rehearsal dinner has a place of great importance within itself and ample time should be allowed for the dinner as this is the time for the two extended families to meet one another as well as all the activities that may surround the event. Often huge sums are spent on rehearsal dinners, in addition to the numbers of guests who have been invited and await the arrival of the wedding party. To have the wedding party arrive late because of lack of promptness at the rehearsal is not in good taste and is easily avoided simply by the director's moving things along.

The Wedding

The Wedding Service itself is the focal point of everything that surrounds the wedding event. The service is the reason for the gathering. The service is why family and friends travel across states and continents to be present. Every effort should be made by every person related to the wedding to ensure that the service is a service of exquisite beauty and dignity, and one that will be remembered by the bride and groom as their most special day.

Arrival

Members of the wedding party should arrive at the site of the wedding in ample time for all necessary preparations with regards to dressing, hair, make-up, photography, etc. Arrival of members of the wedding party should be coordinated with the wedding director. This should be reviewed as one of the final words at the rehearsal.

Room Assignments

Members of the wedding party, including parents and grandparents, should be given room assignments where they may dress and wait until the appointed time for the wedding. The church parlor or Sunday School rooms may serve the purpose if there are no other designated areas. Refreshments in the form of snack food, soft drinks, or water are helpful gestures for making members of the wedding party feel comfortable.

The bride's and groom's rooms should be situated so that there is no visual contact between the two. At the appointed time, the wedding director will come and escort members of the wedding party to their respective locations in order for the wedding to begin.

The Processional

The seating of the mother of the bride, the last of the special guests, usually signals the time for the processional to begin. On the first notes of the processional music, the pastor, groom, and best man enter the sanctuary and take their places in the chancel. As each takes his place, he faces the oncoming members of the procession. The ushers or groomsmen are the first to enter and usually come singly or in pairs and are arranged according to height. The groomsmen usually take their places on the side of the groom, unless they enter escorting the bride's attendants.

Groomsmen are followed by the bride's attendants, followed by the maid/matron of honor. The bridesmaids take their places to the side of the bride. The maid of honor takes her place next to the bride. The ring bearer follows the maid of honor and takes his place near the groom. If there is an aisle runner, two of the groomsmen unroll the runner for the procession of the bride. The flower girl precedes the bride with petals strewn along the way.

Closing the sanctuary doors and changing the processional music offer a mood of grand entrance for the bride. When the sanctuary doors are reopened, the bride and her father or escort enter. This is a grand moment: "the bride's moment." The bride's mother stands as a way of honoring her daughter and the congregation follows.

The Recessional

The congregation should remain seated for the recessional, as a standing congregation blocks the view of some guests. No one should stand until the wedding party and special guests are ushered out.

Wedding Music

Prelude Music for the Organist

Selection	Composer
Adagio Cantabile	G. Tartini
Adagio Cantabile (Violin Sonata #3)	J. S. Bach
Allegro (from Concerto #5)	G. F. Handel, arr. Whitford
Allegro (from Concerto #8)	G. F. Handel, arr. Whitford
Arioso in A (Air on the G. String)	J. S. Bach
Ave Maria	Bach-Gounod, arr. Joyce Jones
Ave Maria	Schubert, arr. Diane Bush
Celebrated Canon in D	J. Pachelbel
Concerto in F Major	G. F. Handel
Jesu, Joy of Man's Desiring	J. S. Bach
Prelude from "The Fairy Queen"	Henry Purcell
Prelude in G Minor	J. S. Bach
Prelude on Rhosymedre	F. J. Haydn
Rondeau from "Abdelazar"	Henry Purcell
Seven Pieces for a Musical Clock	F. J. Haydn
The Faithful Shepherd	G. F. Handel
Voluntary in G	William Walond

Resource Collections for the Organ

Title	Compiler, Editor
Classical Organ Selections	Diane Bush
Favorite Organ Selections	Diane Bush
For Manuals Only	John Christopher
The Biggs Book of Organ Music	E. Powers Biggs
The Diane Bush Wedding Book	Diane Bush
The Oxfords Book of Wedding Music	Oxford

Processional Music for the Organ

Selection	Composer
Air in F Major from "Water Music"	G. F. Handel
Bridal Chorus from "Lohengrin"	Richard Wagner
Canon in D	J. Pachelbel
Grand March from "Aida"	Guiseppe Verdi, arr. B. Hesford
Jesu, Joy of Man's Desiring from Cantata 147	J. S. Bach
Overture from "Music for the Royal Fireworks"	G. F. Handel
Prelude from "Te Deum"	Marc-Antoine Charpentier

Processional — Trumpet Tune in C	Henry Purcell
Processional from "Water Music"	G. F. Handel
Processional in G Major	John Stanley
Psalm XIX	Benedetto Marcello
Psalm XX	Benedetto Marcello
Rigaudon	Andre Campra
Three Trumpet Tunes (C Major, G-Flat, G Major)	David Johnson
Trumpet Tune in D	David Johnson
Trumpet Voluntary in D Major	Henry Purcell
Trumpet Tune in C Major	Henry Purcell
Trumpet Voluntary in D	John Stanley
St. Anthony Chorale	F. J. Haydn
"Prince of Denmark March"	Jeremiah Clarke
Wedding Processional from "The Sound Of Music"	Rodgers and Hammerstein

Recessional Music for the Organ

Selection	Composer
Allegro from "Eine Kleine Nachtmusick"/"A Little Night Music"	W. A. Mozart
Allegro Moderato in D from "Water Music"	G. F. Handel
Allegro Maestoso "Hornpipe" from "Water Music"	G. F. Handel
Entrata Festiva	David Laskey
Fanfare "Pomposo" from "Water Music"	G. F. Handel
Fanfare	J. J. Mouret
Festal Fanfare from Concerto #4	J. S. Bach
Glory to God in the Highest	Giovannie Pergolesi
Joyful, Joyful, We Adore Thee "Ode to Joy"	Ludwig van Beethoven
Let the Merry Bells Ring 'Round	G. F. Handel, arr. Whitfore
Now Thank We All Our God	S. Karg-Elert
Rigadoun	Andre Campra
Spring from "The Four Seasons"	Antonio Vivaldi
Toccata (Fifth Symphony)	Charles Widor
Toccata	Theodore Dubois
Trumpet Allemande	A. Holborne
Trumpet Voluntary	John Stanley
Voluntary in A Major	William Shelby
Wedding March from "A Midsummer Night's Dream"	Felix Mendelssohn

Vocal Solos: Classical/Traditional

Title	Composer
A Wedding Benediction	Austin Lovelace
A Wedding Blessing	Walter Pelz
Ave Maria	J. S. Bach/Charles Gounod

Ave Maria	Franz Shubert
Because	G. d'Hardelot
Bist Du Bei Mir/Be Thou With Me	J. S. Bach
Come Ye Sons of Art	Henry Purcell
Crown with Thy Benediction	G. W. Cassler
Entreat Me Not to Leave Thee from Ruth	Charles Gounod
Gift of Love, Traditional Melody	arr. Hal Hopson
God of Love	Milton Dieterich
God is My Shepherd	Antonin Dvorak
If With All Your Hearts	Felix Mendelssohn
The Lord's Prayer	Albert Hay Malotte
O Father, All Creating	David Fetler
O Perfect Love	Joseph Barney
O Promise Me	R. de Koven
Irish Blessing	Denes Agay
Panis Angelicus/O Lord Most Holy	Cesar Franck
Psalm 23	P. Creston
Song of Devotion	John Ness Beck
The Ring	R. Schumann
The Call	Vaughan Williams
The Greatest of These Is Love	Roberta Bitgood
Wedding Hymn from "Ptolemy"	G. F. Handel
Wedding Song	H. Schuetz
Wedding Song — Psalm 128	Robert Wetzler
Wedding Prayer	David Williams
Wedding Prayer	Fern Glasgow Dunlap
Wedding Song	Flor Peeters
Wedding Processional and Air	J. S. Bach
Where E'er You Walk	G. F. Handel
With This Ring	John Sacco
Wither Thou Goest	Guy Singer

Vocal Solos: Contemporary

Title	Composer
All I Ask of You	Andrew Lloyd Weber
All I Have	Beth Neilson Chapman
Annie's Song	John Denver
Beautiful in My Eyes	Joshua Kadison
Bridal Prayer	Roger Copeland
Butterfly Kisses	Carlisle/Thomas
Double Good to You	Amy Grant
Endless Love	Lionel Richie
Evergreen	Williams

Everything I Do, I Do It For You	Bryan Adams
The Father Says, "I Do"	Brent Lamb
The First Time I Loved Forever	Lee Holdridge
Follow Me	John Denver
From this Moment On	Shania Twain/Bryan White
Grow Old With Me	John Lennon
He Has Chosen You for Me	Pat Terry
How Beautiful	Twila
I Cross My Heart	Steve Dorff and E. Kaz
I Do	Paul Brandt
I'd Build a World in the Heart of a Rose	H. Nicholls
I Swear	Baker
I Will Be There	Steven Curtis Chapman
In This Life	Shamblin
In This Very Room	Ron and Carol Harris
Keeper of the Stars	Mayo and Lee
Love Theme	Paul Johnson
Love Can Build a Bridge	The Judds
The Love That Lasts a Lifetime	Bryan Jeffrey Leech
Me and My House	Tim Sheppard
My Prayer for You	Jimmy Owens
One Hand, One Heart	Leonard Bernstein
On Eagle's Wings	Michael Joncas
Somewhere Out There	Horner, Mann, Weil
That's the Way (With This Ring I Thee Wed)	Public Domain Foundation, Inc.
The Greatest of These Is Love	Bitgood
True Love Comes from God	Jimmy Owens
Turn Around	Harry Belafonte
We've Only Just Begun	Nichols
When I Fall In Love	Victor Young
Wind Beneath My Wings	Gary Morris
You're a Gift	Russell Stevens

Collections

It's Wedding Time	Fred Bock — Singspiration
Whom God Has Joined Together	Fred Bock Music Co.
There's Going to Be a Wedding	Ralph Carmichael, Lexicon Music
The Wedding Album Songbook	Maranatha Music

Sample Wills

Note to the Pastor:

In the chapter titled "Taking Care of Business," the importance of having a couple draw up a will was discussed. Following are sample copies of wills that may be given to a couple for the development of their own wills. These are not copyrighted documents, and pastors should feel free to distribute them and encourage couples to fill them out and make them legal through the signature of witnesses and seal of a notary public.

Sample I

Last Will and Testament of

_____

I, N_____, living at _____
in the State of _____, do make this my last will and
testament and herewith revoke all previous wills that I have previously made. Be it
known that I make this my last will and testament in the state of sound mind and
judgment.

Article One

I will all my tangible property, including household furnishing, automobiles, benefits of insurance policies, bank accounts, securities, stocks, and bonds, to my wife,
N_____, providing that she survives me at the time of my
death. In the event I am not survived by my wife, I will all my said property to my
children to be given in equal shares.

Although I intend no legal obligation on the part of my wife, it is my hope that she
will distribute some of the said property to my children or those in line for their
inheritance as my wife may see appropriate.

Any distribution of my said property to a minor child may be distributed by my
Executrix and/or placed in a trust for the minor until he/she reaches age eighteen
(18) or placed in the keeping of a legal guardian, or some other person selected by
my Executrix.

Article Two

I will and bequeath the remainder of my estate, real and personal, at the time of my
decease, for disposal as follows:

    i.   To my wife, if my wife survives me,
    ii.   To my child(ren) if my wife does not survive me,
    iii.   To my estate for distribution by the Executor/Executrix to my next of
           kin if neither my wife nor child(ren) survive me.

The execution of my will to my next of kin under article iii is declared as follows: Half of my property to my surviving parent(s); and half of my property to be distributed to my surviving siblings.

Article Three

I do, by affixing my signature on this last will and testament, appoint my wife, N_____, to be the guardian of our children who are minor at the time of my death. If I am not survived by my wife at the time of my death or if my wife is unable to serve as guardian, I appoint N_____ of _____ to serve in the stead of my wife.

Article Four

I appoint my wife, N_____, to be the Executrix of this will. In the event my wife, N_____, does not survive me or is unable to serve, I appoint N _____ of _____ to be the Executor/Executrix in her stead.

Article Five

I further will that in addition to the powers given by common or statutory law or any other provisions of this will, my Executrix will have the power without order of the court to retain, sell, divest, or invest any property, real or personal, that I may own at the time of my death.

All taxes, including applicable inheritance taxes, and investment and interest taxes, levied on my estate or bequest shall be paid by my Executrix from the funds of my estate at the time of my death. The Executrix shall not be liable for any losses or damages except as may be caused by her own bad faith. My Executrix may, as deemed appropriate and necessary, consult legal counsel regarding the meaning and implementation of this will.

The empowered duties and authorizations herein given in this will to the Executrix may be exercised by any person succeeding the Executrix in the said office of administration.

Article Six

IN THE WITNESS OF those who have attested my stated LAST WILL AND TES-
TAMENT, I hereby set my hand on this _____ day of _____, 20___.

_____
Signature

We, the signed and declared witnesses, do affix our signatures
To this Last Will and Testament for:

N_____

At his request, and in his presence, and in the presence of each other, this

_____ *day of* _____, *20___.*

_____   _____

_____   _____
(Name and address of witness)   *(Name and address of witness)*

COUNTY: _____

STATE: _____

Subscribed and sworn before me by the testator and the said
Witnesses, on this _____ day of _____, 20____.

_____
Notary Public

My commission expires: _____

Sample II

Last Will and Testament

of

_____

_____

State

_____

County

I, N_____, of _____ (*Street Address, City, County, State*), being of sound mind and memory, but considering the uncertainty of life and the certainty of death, and desiring while living to make provision for the disposition of my worldly goods after my death, do make and declare this my Last Will and Testament, hereby revoking and declaring void any and all Wills which I have made heretofore.

ITEM ONE

I direct that all my just debts, funeral expenses, cost of administration of my estate, and taxes that may be due be paid out of the assets of my estate as soon as might be possible after my death.

ITEM TWO

I give, devise, and bequeath all the property which I may own at the time of my death, real and personal, tangible and intangible, of whatever kind and wherever situated, including all property which I may acquire or become entitled to after the execution of this Will, to my wife, N_____.

ITEM THREE

In the event of a common disaster or if my said wife is not living at the time of my death, then and in that event, I give, devise, and bequeath all my property to my child(ren), N_____ and N_____, who shall equally share in the values of the estate. If either child is not living, I give, devise, bequeath his/her equal share of my estate to his/her surviving spouse. In the latter case, it is my will that fifty per cent (50%) of that said portion of my estate be held in trust for each child of that spouse who was parented by my son/daughter until that child reaches the age of eighteen (18).

ITEM FOUR

If at the time of my death, neither my said wife, nor any child of mine, nor any spouse child of a child of mine, nor any child of a child of mine, nor any descendant of mine, is living, then in that event, I give, devise, and bequeath my estate to my siblings, including, N_____, N_____, and N_____. If at that said time, non of my siblings are living, I instruct that my estate be given to N_____ charity for distribution of the funds as deemed appropriate by the trustees of the charity.

ITEM FIVE

I hereby appoint my wife, N_____, the Executrix of this my Last Will and Testament. I hereby grant unto my Executrix the absolute, discretionary power to deal with any property, real or personal, held in my estate, as freely as I might in the handling of my own affairs. I direct the Executrix named herein not be required to furnish bond in the performance of her duties. In the event that my said wife should not be living at the time of my death or otherwise be unable to serve, then and in that event, I appoint N_____ as Executor/Exectutrix of this my last Will. I also further direct that he/she not be required to furnish bond and shall have the same powers and duties set out above.

IN TESTIMONY WHEREOF, I, N_____, have here-unto set my hand and seal, and publish and declare this to be my Last Will and Testament, in the presence of the witnesses named below, this _____ day of _____, 20_____.

_____
                           Full Name

Signed, sealed, published, and declared by the said N_____ to be his Last Will and Testament in the presence of us, who, at his request, and in his presence, and in the presence of each other, do subscribe our names as witnesses thereto.

Witness _____

Address _____

Witness _____

Address _____

Notary Public _____

                       Commission No _____

                       Commission Expires: _____

Letters from the Pastor

Receiving personal letters from the pastor who has been called upon to perform the wedding ceremony creates an even greater bond between the pastor and the respective couple. No pastor should ever underestimate the meaning conveyed to a couple in their receiving a personal letter from their pastor. Following are several sample letters which pastors using this sourcebook are welcome to use, either as they appear in the sourcebook or as may be adapted for their own particular needs. Pastors should feel free to use these letters as they see fit.

1. On Receiving News of the Engagement

Date

Inside Address

Dear N_____ and N_____,

    I just learned of your engagement and wanted to write and extend my congratulations to the two of you. What a very special time this is in your lives as you stand on tiptoe and look joyfully to the future. I am sure wonderful things are awaiting the two of you, and having known the two of you for some time, I know you deserve the very best.

    Marriage is a huge step and you have no doubt given it the serious consideration that it deserves. Engagement is both a time of joy and anticipation. It is a time to dream, to set goals, and to plan, not only for your wedding, but for the marriage that is to follow.

    I am sure everyone in your two families is very excited with the news that you have recently shared regarding your engagement and upcoming marriage. Please know that your church family and I, as your pastor, also rejoice with you in this exciting news and look forward to working with you in any way I can be of support and service. I would like to meet with you at your convenience to share further with you regarding your upcoming wedding and to lend my support in every way possible.

    May God bless you during these days of engagement and preparation for your upcoming marriage.

In Christ's abundant love,

Rev. N_____, Pastor

2. To the Newly Married Couple

Date

Inside Address

Dear N_____ and N_____,

First, congratulations on your marriage!! Your wedding ceremony was beautiful, and I feel certain that everyone who attended felt uplifted not only by the beauty of the ceremony, but by the sincerity with which you spoke your vows. I must share with you that I was quite moved as I looked into your eyes as you shared your vows with one another. It was most apparent that your words were spoken from the heart and the bond you made was sealed with a commitment that cannot be broken.

Thank you for allowing me to be a part of this meaningful service. Not only was I personally blessed by having the honor of being the officiating pastor, but I have felt inspired by the many compliments I have received on the service. From all the words of praise that I received from many of the people who attended the service, I know that the service was not only a blessing to you, but to your family and friends as well. Realizing that a service like yours penetrates the hearts of so many makes it an even greater blessing, if such is possible!

You are such a fine couple and getting to know you during our premarital interviews as we were planning your wedding underscored for me yet again how fortunate I am to know a couple like you. I know wonderful things are in store for the two of you as you travel your life's journey together. How could they be otherwise?

I am certain you enjoyed your wedding trip and are ready to begin finding the fulfillment of the dreams that you shared as we talked about your lives together. May the Spirit of Christ be near and dear to you each day. Please know that I am here for you as your pastor and friend. Whatever help I can ever give, please do not hesitate to call.

With love and prayer,

Rev. N_____, Pastor

3. To the Parents of the Bride

Date:

Inside Address

Dear N_____ and N_____,

What an honor it was to have been a part of N_____'s wedding. Thank you for allowing me to share in the joy of this beautiful event. I wanted to write and not only express my pleasure in officiating at your daughter's wedding, but also to tell you what an outstanding young lady N_____ is. In the premarital interviews that we were able to share and the other times that we were able to talk, it became more and more apparent what an outstanding person she is and what a fine job you have done as parents in bringing her up with the values she holds.

I also wanted to tell you what a beautiful wedding it was. The beauty of it was not only in the chancel setting, the elegant floral arrangements, or the wedding party, but more particularly in the sincerity of the exchange of the vows, the love and support that surrounded this couple from their family and friends, and the feeling that everyone had that they were truly on their way to a beautiful and wonderful life. There are many things about ministry that bless a pastor's heart, but the experience of officiating at such an event as a beautiful and meaningful wedding certainly stands at the top of the list.

It is my opinion that no child ever becomes what they become by accident. Like a vessel in a potter's hand, they are molded from the moment of birth through the years to become who they are. You have been most devoted parents and have instilled in N_____ values that will make her not only a good wife, but also a person of quality in every way. May the spirit of Christ bless and use her and N_____ in the days ahead that their home may be a haven of happiness and a place of peace.

In the love and ministry of Christ,

Rev. N_____, Pastor

4. Letter to the Parents of the Groom

Date

Inside Address

Dear N_____ and N_____,

What a pleasure it was to be a part of your son's wedding and to have the opportunity to get to know him. In preparation for their marriage, I came to appreciate both N_____ and N_____ and the values they hold for themselves and their marriage. The wedding was truly one of beauty and inspiration. I often think of all the things that make a wedding beautiful: the church, the floral arrangements, the bridal party, the music, and the service itself. When all is said and done, I believe it is the sincerity of the couple and the expression of love they have for one another. That was so apparent in your son's wedding, and such an affirmation will be the solid foundation for the future they will share.

I also wanted to tell you what a fine son you have. Not only will he be a good husband, but I am sure a quality person in every respect. I have often said that nothing ever happens by accident, and I know that is true of our children. It takes years of dedicated effort to make them into the kinds of devoted people that I found your son to be. You are to be commended as parents, for I can see that he is a reflection of your values and character.

There are many blessings in the life of a minister, but I believe the opportunity to officiate in a wedding is one of the greater blessings. This was certainly the case with your son and his lovely wife. I know they are on their way to a life filled with good things and a life of purpose. You can be very proud.

Yours in Christ's loving service,

Rev. N_____, Pastor

5. Letter to the Couple on their First Christmas

Date

Inside address

Dear N_____ and N_____,

It is hard to believe that another Christmas is here as so much has happened during the past year, but in just a couple of weeks we will be celebrating that most blessed of events. I was just thinking about the two of you and that this will be your first Christmas as husband and wife. Holidays are always special, but I sometimes think that our "first holidays" as a married couple have even greater meaning as the two of you will be sharing the joys of holiday together.

Your wedding was only a few months ago and the memory of it still lingers and simply remembering it gives you joy. I must say that it was a very beautiful wedding, but even more than remembering the wedding, I remember what a special couple the two of you are. It was a pleasure to get to know you in the interviews we had in preparing you for marriage and planning the wedding itself. It was an honor to be the officiating pastor at such a beautiful event and to hear your vows. I distinctly remember how you spoke your vows with such meaning.

As you celebrate your first Christmas, please know that I am thinking of you and remembering you in prayer that the presence of the Savior born in Bethlehem will be especially near and dear to you. You are a special couple! May God hold you always in his care.

In the spirit of Christmas,

Rev. N_____, Pastor

6. On the First Wedding Anniversary

Date

Inside address

Dear N_____ and N_____,

Can you believe it has been a year since your wedding? Wow, how time passes! I am quite sure that this has been a most special year for the two of you as you have begun your life's journey together.

I have thought of you often during the past year. Yours was such a beautiful and memorable wedding. No doubt you have relived those moments many times as you have reflected on the service and all the events that surrounded it. You are such an outstanding couple, and it was a pleasure to get to know you during the weeks that preceded your wedding. I also remember your families, and just as you are proud of them, I am confident they are very proud of you and what you are making of your lives.

It has been said that love grows stronger over the years. You are no doubt experiencing the truth of that saying. Just think where your relationship will be five or ten years from now in terms of the bond between the two of you. You may be wondering if it can get any better than this! Well, I am confident God has wonderful things in store for you.

As you celebrate your first anniversary, please know that you are in my thoughts and held in prayer that God will continue to bless and uphold you and surround you with his presence. God bless.

Faithfully yours,

Rev. N_____, Pastor

7. On the Birth of a Child

Date

Inside Address

Dear N_____ and N_____,

Congratulations on the birth of your new baby! What an exciting time this must be in your lives, and I know both of you are jumping for joy. As you have held N_____ in your arms, you must truly feel there is no joy that can exceed what you are feeling as new parents. Children are truly a gift from God.

It seems like such a short time ago that we were celebrating your beautiful wedding and now you are celebrating this wonderful blessing. Perhaps you remember our conversation about "two becoming as one." There is no where in a marriage where this is more pronounced than in the gift of children. Your child is the extension of the two of you and the love you have found in one another. He/she will resemble the two of you in so many ways: personality, appearance, even expressions. You can truly rejoice that in the birth of this little one, two have literally become as one. What a blessing beyond measure!

The congregation shares with me in extending you our congratulations and best wishes. We look forward to all the opportunities of surrounding you and your new little one with our love and prayers. Be well assured that our nursery attendant will take the very best of care of him/her when you feel ready to return to church.

We thank God for this child and for the ever new possibilities which lie open to him/her as a child of God. May God watch over him/her and you each day.

In the service of the One who said, "Let the little children come unto me,"

Rev. N_____ , Pastor

8. Letter Inviting Non-member Spouse to Join Church

Date

Inside Address

Dear N_____,

It was such an honor to have been a part of your and N_____'s wedding. I have heard many comments from your family and friends who attended regarding what a truly beautiful and meaningful event it was. No doubt everyone felt as I did, that it was indeed a very, very special wedding.

During the course of our premarital interviews, we had discussed the benefits of your attending and participating in the same church. I am happy to see that you have been attending here as well as joining in some of the activities and programs associated with the church. I trust these, as well as the worship services themselves, are a source of blessing in your life.

We would love to have you join our church through a transfer of membership, and I write this letter to offer that invitation officially. As I am certain you have already experienced, this is not only a very friendly congregation, but also one with exciting programs that offer newly-married couples many opportunities for participation. Our membership class will be meeting _Date and Time_ and we would love to have you come and learn more about the church and consider making this your church home. Please give me a call if you have any questions.

Again, thank you for your participation in the church services. It is always good to see you.

Yours in Christ's service,

Rev. N_____, Pastor

Part V

**Resources
for the Couple**

Resources for the Couple

The Engagement

Engagement is a time not only for couples to get to know one another better, but also for making plans toward the wedding and future marriage. It is a "pre-commitment" to the espoused and the time when the marital covenant will be formally made. Many events transpire during the time of engagement, including preparations for the wedding, planning the wedding trip, planning for establishment of a home, engagement parties and wedding showers, meetings with the pastor, wedding director, and music director, and attending to numerous details that crop up in the process of planning.

Families First

Normally, families should be the first to know of one's engagement and plans for the upcoming wedding. The manner in which this news is shared varies from couple to couple. Sharing the exciting news with the couple's parents and families not only offers an opportunity for these special people to share the joy and excitement, it also affords them the time-honored courtesy that they, the most important people in one's life, were the first to know.

Informing families first does several things:

- Informing them first enables them to process the news before it is spread to the wider circle of extended family and friends.

- Informing them first gains their support and input.

- Informing them first removes any worry or anxiety that they may hear the news from someone else. Such would be a travesty.

- Informing them first enables them to begin making plans regarding their involvement and calendar.

The manner of informing parents is one of personal preference. However, like the announcement of any event of importance, a little planning will enhance and elevate the joy of sharing the news. Such a sharing will always be remembered and appreciated by parents and in-laws and will further ensure that the new relationship is getting off to a great beginning. The announcement should never be made "casually." Like any announcement of importance, it should be done at a carefully appointed time and place. While it doesn't have to be elaborate, setting a "time to talk" will accentuate the entire process in an unbelievable way. Here are a few suggestions couples may consider:

- The couple may inform the parents they have some news they would like to share and would like to make an appointment to talk.

- The couple may prepare a dinner for the parents and in the process of invitation, inform the parents they have some news they would like to share.

- The couple may take their parents out to dinner at some favorite place and during the dinner share the exciting news.

- The couple may invite both sets of parents to a special setting and inform both at the same time.

- The couple may bring a bouquet of flowers, balloons, or any thing that sets a festive mood to the appointed place of announcement to make sharing the news celebrative and memorable.

Publishing the News

Once the couple has decided to make the news of the engagement known, it is customary to make the announcement formally in the newspaper. Newspapers have different requirements regarding engagement announcements. Usually there is an engagement form that is sent to the bride requesting information about the engagement and upcoming wedding, along with a request for a picture either of the bride-to-be or of the engaged couple. Some newspapers charge a fee for publishing engagement announcements and others do it as a public service. The society editor is the contact person at the newspaper.

The advantage of making a formal announcement in the newspaper is to inform the public of the upcoming wedding. This not only shares the news, but enables people who need to be thinking ahead in terms of the family calendar and plans.

In addition to announcing the news through the newspaper, the couple may wish to make the announcement through announcement cards to special friends and family. This added touch makes the recipients feel quite special that they were singled out to be recipients of this special news.

Wedding Gifts

Wedding gifts not only are a way to provide for the basic needs of a couple starting a new home, but also serve as tokens of love and friendship. Family and friends want to honor the couple with gifts as a way of expressing their love and support for the marriage.

It is important to keep accurate records of who has given what gifts. Since no bride wishes to fail to acknowledge the gift or the gift giver, it is important to keep accurate records to avoid mix-ups. A booklet to record each gift, the giver, and the store from which it came (in case it has to be exchanged), and the date of its arrival will help avoid any embarrassing mistakes. Gifts may be numbered with a sticker and corresponding name.

Registering for Gifts

Registering preferences with a store's wedding gift registry is a courtesy to friends in that it spares them the time of gift hunting for the perfect gift as well as avoiding duplications for gifts or disappointments of giving gifts that are not needed.

Thank You Notes

Thank you notes are important in that they acknowledge to the giver the gift has been received. Thank you notes need not be long, but should be personal and handwritten, and the gift given should be mentioned in the note. In order that a backlog of unwritten notes not accumulate, it is a good idea to begin writing thank you notes soon after the first wedding gifts are received.

Displaying Wedding Gifts

Friends enjoy admiring wedding gifts. Setting up a display table in one's home to show the gifts is a way of sharing the joy and gratitude of the gifts received.

Wedding Customs

Engagement Ring

The engagement or betrothal ring dates back to the days when marriage was made by arrangement or "purchase." The ring was viewed as a partial payment for the bride or as a symbol of the groom's honorable intentions. Diamonds were introduced as a symbol of enduring love.

Wedding Ring

The wedding ring is circular and suggests the unending love of the giver. The giving of wedding rings goes back to the days of the early Egyptians who gave the one married a ring as a sign of love, honor, and betrothal. The wedding ring is worn on the third finger of the left hand which was believed to have a vein connected directly to the heart.

Wedding Veil

In ancient times and in some cultures today, the wedding veil symbolizes youth, purity, and modesty. While the veil is white in weddings today, historically it has been darker colors completely covering most of the face. In some cultures today the groom meets the bride veiled and never sees her face until after the wedding.

Wearing of White

White is the color of purity. The wearing of white symbolizes the bride has been "undefiled," and is awaiting consummation of the marriage by the one to whom she is betrothed. White has also been the symbol of celebration since Roman times. The color of white today maintains the meaning of happiness and joy.

Bridal Flowers

The tradition of the bride carrying flowers dates back to early Roman times when brides carried bunches of herbs under their veils to represent fidelity. Ivy carried by brides among the ancient Greeks was a sign of indissoluble love. Flowers have long stood for a variety of emotions and values, such as lilies for virtue and roses for love.

The tossing of the bridal bouquet to the single women symbolizes the hope that they, too, will have the good fortune of meeting a special person who will bring the same joy and love to their lives as the groom has to the bride's.

Rice and Petals

Tossing rice on the newly married couple is an Oriental tradition that symbolized fertility and good fortune. In recent years, the tossing of rice has been replaced by the tossing of flower petals which symbolize beauty, joy, and prosperity.

Bridal Aisle Runner

Having the bride walk on the white aisle runner is an ancient tradition that represents her walking on holy ground. The marriage is not merely witnessed by the gathered guests, but is a covenant made in the presence of God himself. The white aisle runner represents God's holiness and presence on which the bride advances toward the holy covenant between her and her beloved.

Reserved Seating for Parents

Parents occupy a place of honor in the lives of their children. Parents are a part of the marriage ceremony and the commitments they make are also binding commitments. An enormous transition takes place during the wedding service as a new family is formed. Parents enter in the line of authority and leave in the line of support of the new family.

Clasping Right Hands

The right hand is the symbol of strength, trust, and support. In clasping the right hand, couples are doing far more than simply joining hands. They are expressing their commitment of strength, trust, and support and sealing that contract in the joining of hands.

The Bridal Kiss

Historically, a kiss meant far more than the show of affection. In the wedding, it also connotes a much deeper meaning. In the early days of the church, the Apostle Paul said that Christians should greet one another with a kiss. In Roman times, the kiss was symbolic of a legal bond. The kiss has transitioned into part of the marriage ceremony as a seal of the sacred bond.

Pronouncement of Husband and Wife

Traditionally the pastor has pronounced the couple as "Husband and Wife." Using the word, husband, first was symbolic of the change of names and the beginning of a new life. In recent times, some ceremonies pronounce the couple "Wife and Husband," characteristic of the changing times when women have more egalitarian roles. In some marriages, women now keep their maiden names or hyphenate their own names with that of their husband.

Signing the License

The signing of the legal documents by the bride and groom, the pastor, and the witnesses establishes public documentation of the legality of the marriage.

Sharing the Wedding Cake

The practice of the bride and groom feeding each other the wedding cake implies the coming together of their lives as one. In the New Testament this symbolism of oneness in sharing the bread was the Lord's Supper.

Signing the Guest Register

Guests should always sign the guest register as it represents not only their presence at the wedding, but that they were in fact witnesses to the wedding. Signing the guest register is a practice that began among the ancient Greeks as an indication that they as guest bore witness to the wedding vows.

Receiving Line

The Receiving Line is a part of the wedding itself. Although not an official part of the ceremony, it allows guests to offer their love and blessing to the newly-wed couple.

Planning Checklist

No one, including the pastor, fully understands all that is involved in planning a wedding until he/she has gone through the process. There is far more to do than meets the eye and it is easy to overlook any number of concerns. The following checklist will enable couples to move through the process more easily.

Announcements

_____ The families of the bride and groom have been informed of the engagement and the upcoming wedding.

_____ The newspapers in which the engagement is to be announced have been informed. Newspapers have different guidelines so each paper should be contacted and an engagement announcement form secured.

_____ Announcement has been made to expended family members and special friends.

Scheduling of Dates/Reservations

_____ The date and time for the wedding has been set.

_____ The wedding date and time has been calendared in on the church calendar.

_____ Any reservation fees for use of the church have been paid.

_____ The initial meeting with the pastor has been held.

_____ The initial meeting with the Wedding Director has been held.

Resource People

_____ The premarital counseling sessions with the pastor have been scheduled.

_____ The organist/accompanist/music director has/have been contacted and an initial meeting held.

_____ The vocalist(s) and/or instrumentalist(s) has/have been contacted.

_____ The florist has been selected.

_____ The photographer has been contacted and secured.

_____ The videographer (if used) has been contacted and secured.

_____ The caterer for the reception has been secured.

_____ Master of Ceremonies for the rehearsal dinner has been secured.

_____ Band or Disc Jockey for rehearsal dinner has been booked.

_____ Band or Disc Jockey for wedding reception has been booked.

_____ Limousine (if used) and other special transportation have been reserved.

Checklist for the Bride and her Family

_____ The maid/matron of honor has been chosen and confirmed.

_____ The bride's attendants have been chosen and confirmed.

_____ The flower girl(s) has/have been chosen and confirmed.

_____ The Gift Registry has been set up in appropriate stores.

_____ A record of gifts has been properly kept.

_____ Gifts have been properly displayed.

_____ Thank you notes for gifts have been written.

_____ Invitations to the wedding have been ordered.

_____ A Wedding Guests list (in consultation with the groom and his family) has been developed.

_____ Invitations to the wedding have been addressed and mailed.

_____ The bride's dress has been ordered and properly fitted.

_____ The attendants' dresses have been ordered and properly fitted.

_____ Bouquets/corsages for attendants and flower girls have been ordered.

_____ A site has been chosen for the reception.

_____ Have met with the chosen caterer and decided on menu and serving arrangements.

_____ Have met with the emcee of the reception and reviewed format of reception including introductions, music, dances, etc.

_____ Special music requested has been given to organist/vocalist.

_____ Arrangements have been made for dressing the bride and attendants before the wedding.

_____ Have arranged for payment of custodian, organist, instrumentalist, vocalist.

_____ Flowers for the wedding and reception site have been ordered.

_____ Engagement picture and bride's portrait have been made.

_____ Transportation to wedding and reception sites has been arranged.

_____ Wedding ring for groom has been bought.

_____ Gifts for the bride's attendants have been purchased.

_____ Lodging arrangements have been made for out-of-town attendants.

_____ Lodging information has been sent to out-of-town guests.

_____ Wedding announcements and bride's (or couple's) wedding picture have been sent to desired newspapers. Newspapers will send proper forms and cost requirements.

_____ Wedding bulletins (if to be used in service) have been ordered and service information obtained from officiating pastor _____, organist _____, vocalists _____, instrumentalist(s) _____.

_____ Unity Candle (if used) ordered or purchased.

_____ A date for the bridesmaid luncheon has been set.

_____ A place for the bridesmaid luncheon has been reserved.

_____ The menu for the bridesmaid luncheon has been confirmed.

_____ Invitations for the bridesmaid luncheon have been sent.

Checklist for the Groom and His Family

_____ The place of the rehearsal dinner has been decided and reservations made.

_____ The menu for the rehearsal dinner has been chosen.

_____ The format of the rehearsal dinner has been decided: emcee, music, toasts, introductions, seating, head table, theme.

_____ A band or DJ for the rehearsal dinner has been chosen and confirmed.

_____ Invitations to the rehearsal dinner have been ordered.

_____ Invitations to the rehearsal dinner have been mailed.

_____ The bride's ring(s) have been purchased.

_____ The best man has been chosen and confirmed.

_____ The groomsmen have been chosen and confirmed.

_____ Gifts for the groomsmen have been purchased.

_____ The ring bearer (if any) has been chosen and confirmed.

_____ Tuxedo (if used) for the groom has been ordered.

_____ Tuxedos (if used) for the groomsmen and ring bearer have been ordered.

_____ Arrangements have been made for dressing at the wedding site.

_____ Arrangements have been made for the honorarium for the person conducting the ceremony.

_____ Bride's flowers, including going away corsage, have been ordered. (This should be done in conjunction with the florist.)

_____ Lodging for out-of-town groomsmen has been arranged.

_____ All reservations for the wedding trip:

  _____ First night's lodging

  _____ Transportation (including gratuities)

_____   Destination, events, and activities

_____   Return trip home

Checklist for the Bride and Groom

_____   All requirements for scheduling the church have been met.

_____   The premarital counseling schedule with the officiating pastor is complete.

_____   The marriage license has been procured. (This may be obtained from the Clerk of Court's Office in any given county and may be used only in that county, or some are good for the entire state. Couples should be so advised. License is usually good for thirty to sixty days, depending on the state. Some states have physical exam or blood test requirements prior to obtaining the license.)

Responsibilities of Wedding Party Members

Conveying information to individual members of the wedding party may be made easier simply by sending each responsible member an informational card outlining his or her responsibilities. This will not only ensure that the particular person understands his/her responsibility, but also confirms to the bridal couple that those responsible understand their respective responsibilities. Responsibilities of the key members of the wedding party are as follows:

Maid/Matron of Honor

- Holds a bridal shower for the bride.
- May offer a toast at rehearsal dinner.
- Assists bride with needful concerns, such as addressing invitations.
- Assists bride dressing for the wedding.
- Arranges brides veil and dress before the processional.
- Holds bride's bouquet during service.
- If there is no ring bearer, holds groom's ring during service.
- Is presented at the reception.
- Stands next to the bride in the receiving line.
- Dances with the best man at the wedding reception.
- Assists bride in changing in preparation for wedding trip.
- Signs marriage license.

Best Man

- Initiates and organizes bachelor's party.
- Offers toast at the rehearsal dinner.
- Drives groom to the place of the wedding.
- Brings marriage license to the wedding if it has not been given to pastor.
- Gives honorarium to pastor and other service providers at the day of the wedding.
- Holds the bride's ring if there is no ring bearer.
- Signs the marriage license as a witness.
- Is presented at the reception.
- Offers the first toast at the reception.
- Dances with the maid/matron of honor.
- May drive couple to the place of their departure for their wedding trip.
- Oversees the return of groomsmen's rented apparel.

Bridesmaids

- Help maid of honor with the bridal shower.
- Participate in pre-wedding bridal parties.
- May offer toasts at the rehearsal dinner.
- Participate in the bridal processional.

- Are presented at the reception.
- Form part of the receiving line.
- Dance with the groomsmen at the reception.
- Gather the unmarried guests for the bridal bouquet toss.
- See the bridal couple off.

Groomsmen

- Support the best man with responsibilities at the bachelor's party.
- May offer toasts at the rehearsal dinner.
- Serve as ushers for the wedding guests by giving out wedding programs, if a receptionist is not available, and seating guests.
- Pull aisle runner down the aisle.
- Direct guests to reception site.
- Are presented at the reception.
- Dance with bridesmaids and other guests.

Mother of the Bride

- Supports bride in preparing guests list.
- Helps with the planning of the wedding and reception.
- Assists bride with the selection of the wedding dress.
- Aids bride in keeping up with wedding gifts, displaying gifts, and thank you notes.
- Assists bride's out-of-town guests with accommodations.
- Is the last to be seated for wedding.
- Stands as a signal for all guests to stand on the entrance of the bride.
- Is presented at the reception.
- Stands beside husband and is the first couple in the receiving line.
- Dances with the groom after the first dance at the reception.
- Acts as hostess at the reception.

Father of the Bride

- Offers toast at the rehearsal dinner.
- Accompanies his daughter in the ride to the wedding site.
- Escorts the bride down the aisle and gives her away on behalf of family.
- Sits with wife after giving daughter away.
- Is presented at the reception.
- Stands with wife as the first couple in the receiving line.
- Dances with the bride after the first dance.
- Acts as host at the reception.

Mother of the Groom

- Helps make accommodations for groom's out-of-town guests.
- Plans rehearsal dinner in conjunction with father of the groom.
- Is next to the last seated for the wedding.
- Is presented at the reception.
- Stands with husband as the second couple in the receiving line.

Father of the Groom

- With groom's mother, helps plan rehearsal dinner.
- Welcomes guests to the rehearsal dinner.
- Introduces head table.
- May serve as emcee at rehearsal dinner if no other emcee is selected.
- Offers toast to bride and groom at rehearsal dinner.

Financial Responsibilities

The question of who is responsible to pay for what expenses of the wedding is a commonly asked question. Having a checklist stating who is responsible for various costs avoids misunderstandings. Traditionally, the groom and his family are responsible for the rehearsal dinner while the bride's family is responsible for the wedding ceremony and the reception that follows. The couple themselves or the groom's parents may offer to contribute to this cost if they so choose. Most marriage books of etiquette divide the expenses of the wedding in the following manner:

The Bride and Her Family

- Invitations and announcements
- Wedding dress and accessories
- Bouquets or corsages for attendants and flower girl
- Flowers for the ceremony and reception sites
- Engagement and wedding photography
- Rental fee (if any) from the church
- Fees for the custodian, organist, instrumentalist, vocalist
- Rental of all equipment pertaining to the wedding service
- Transportation of the bridal party to the wedding and receptions sites
- Reception, including food, beverages, music, gratuities, and professional services
- Wedding ring for the groom
- Gifts for the bride's attendants
- Lodging cost, (if needed) for any out-of-town attendants for the bride

The Groom and His Family

- Bride's engagement and wedding ring
- Marriage license
- The rehearsal dinner, including site, menu, invitations
- Honorarium for the person performing the ceremony
- Bride's flowers, including going away corsage
- Lodging cost for out-of-town groomsmen
- Cost of the wedding trip

Great Wedding Resources and Planners

A wealth of wedding information and ideas may be obtained through the internet. Two of the most prominent websites are: The Knot and The Wedding Zone. Listed below are the website addresses for both. Simply clicking on the site will bring loads of information and creative ideas.

1. The Knot: www.theknot.com

2. The Wedding Zone: www.weddingzone.net

Endnote References

1. This section developed in consultation with Carol Winn of BB&T (Branch Banking & Trust Company), Newton, North Carolina, August, 2002.

2. Daniel Freeman, "Why Get Married?" *Theology News and Notes of Fuller Theological Seminary,* December, 1973, p. 117.

3. *Book of Common Worship* (Louisville, Kentucky: Westminster/John Knox Press, 1993), used by permission.

4. *Book of Worship United Church of Christ* (New York: United Church of Christ Office of Church Life and Leadership, 1986), used by permission.

5. "A Baptist Service of Worship," developed by Ed Yount, Conover, North Carolina, used by permission.

6. "Services of Worship," *United Methodist Book of Worship* (The United Methodist Publishing House, 1979, 1980, 1989, 1992), used by permission, all rights reserved.

7. The Canon Law Society of America, Catholic University of America, 1985, reprinted by permission.

8. James Coriden, Thomas Green, and Donald Heintschel, *The Code of Canon Law, Text and Commentary* (J. J. Mahwah: Paulist Press, 1985), p. 740, used by permission.

9. The Canon Law Society of America.

10. *Ibid.*

11. Coriden, p. 744.

12. The Canon Law Society of America.

13. *Ibid.*

14. Coriden, p. 752.

15. The Canon Law Society of America.

16. "The Chancery," Diocese of Charlotte, Charlotte, North Carolina.

17. The Canon Law Society of America.

18. Consultation with Father James Collins, St. Joseph Catholic Church, Newton, North Carolina, August, 2002.

19. "Ask a Rabbi on Jewish Community on Line," Life Cycle Events: Weddings, www.jewish.com.

20. David K. Shipler, *A Country of Strangers, Blacks and Whites in America* (New York: Alfred A. Knopf), 1997, p. 117, used by permission.

21. *Ibid.*, p. 117.

22. *Ibid.*, p. 112.

23. *Ibid.*, p. 72.

24. *Ibid.*, p. 80.

Lightning Source UK Ltd.
Milton Keynes UK
UKHW051412100920
369582UK00002B/15